Full Circle

Full Circle
Bringing up Children in the Post-Permissive Society
Edited by Digby Anderson

Published by The Social Affairs Unit

41408

306.85 B0001498

British Library Cataloguing in Publication Data

Full circle? : bringing up children in the
post-permissive society.
1. Families – Sociological perspectives
I. Anderson, Digby, C., *1944–*
306.8′5

ISBN 0–907631–29–0

Book production by Crowley Esmonde Ltd
Typeset in Times by TJB Photosetting Ltd., South Witham,
Lincolnshire
Printed and bound in Great Britain by SRP Ltd., Exeter

Contents

The Authors:

Dr. Digby Anderson is Director of the Social Affairs Unit. He is author and contributing editor of sixteen books and reports including *Evaluating Curriculum Proposals*, *Health Education in Practice*, *The Ignorance of Social Intervention*, *The Kindness that Kills* and *Family Portraits*. He has contributed many articles to journals and periodicals including *Poetics Today*, *Journal of Social Policy*, *Economic Affairs*, and *Philosophy of the Social Sciences*. He is a regular columnist in *The Times* and *The Spectator*.

Christopher Brand is a differential psychologist at the University of Edinburgh. His chief interests are in indentifying and understanding the major dimensions of human psychological variation (eg. his review in *Psychological Survey*, Vol. 5). He contributed chapters on political attitudes and on intelligence to the recent edited volumes *Hans Eysenck* and *Arthur Jensen*. He is a Fellow of the Eugenics Society.

Professor Richard Lynn is a Professor of Psychology at the University of Ulster. He is the author of *Arousal, Attention and the Orientation Reaction*, *The Universities and the Business Community*, *The Irish Brain Drain*, *Personality and National Character*, *Introduction to the Study of Personality* and *Educational Achievement in Japan: Lessons for the West*. He edited *The Entrepreneur* and *Dimensions of Personality* and has contributed many articles to journals of psychology and social science.

Errol Mathura is an Adviser in Community Education. He is currently researching into policy-making and falling rolls. His publications include articles in *Journal of European Industrial Training* and *Youth In Society*. He also contributed a chapter in *Adult Education and the Youth Service*.

Professor David Marsland teaches in the Department of Human Sciences and researches in the Institute of Organisation and Social Studies at Brunel University. His many publications include *Sociological Explorations in the Service of Youth*, and *Issues and Methods in Social Education*. He is co-author with Ralph Segalman of *From Cradle to Grave: Perspectives on the State of Welfare* (forthcoming) and editor of *Education and Youth*.

Dr. Barbara Pickard is an Honorary Research Fellow in the Department of Animal Physiology and Nutrition at Leeds University. She is author of *Eating Well for a Healthy Pregnancy* and contributed a chapter to *A Diet of Reason: Sense and Nonsense in the Healthy Eating Debate*. She has lectured and written extensively on nutrition for both the popular and scientific press.

Professor Richard Whitfield is Honorary Chairman of the National Campaign for the Family and a former Director of Child Care (UK) for the Save the Children Fund. He is Professor Emeritus of Education at Aston University and Reader in Advanced Studies at the Gloucester College of Arts and Technology. He is author of *Education for Family Life: some new policies for child care* and his last book, *Families Matter*, was a timely reminder to parents and politicians of the need for coherent family policies if children and those who care for them are to thrive.

Patricia Morgan was Research Fellow in Socio-Legal Studies at the London School of Economics from 1979 to 1982. Her books include *Child Care: Sense and Fable*, *Delinquent Phantasies* and chapters in the collections *Criminal Welfare on Trial* and *Family Portraits*. She is currently researching into the politics of the family. She is a regular contributor to academic journals and periodicals and has also written for *The Daily Telegraph*.

Lynette Burrows has six children of her own, was a registered childminder and ran a play group for seven years. She now teaches part-time. Her book *Good Children* resulted in her being jointly nominated as 'Catholic Woman of the Year' in 1986. She has contributed articles on education, child-rearing and life as a committed mother

6

to magazines and newspapers. She is currently writing a book on motherhood.

Dr. Mervyn Hiskett was Vice-Principal of the School for Arabic Studies in Cano, Nigeria from 1951–62; Lecturer in Hausa Studies, University of London School of Oriental and African Studies, 1962–1981; Visiting Professor in Hausa Studies, Bayero University, Cano, 1981–1983 and Professor of Hausa Studies at the University of Sokoto, Nigeria from 1983 until his retirement in 1985.

Dr. Gerry Mulhern taught psychology at the University of Edinburgh from 1981 to 1984, before moving to his present position as lecturer in psychology at the University of Ulster. He is an Associate of the British Psychological Society and a member of the International Group for the Psychology of Mathematics Education. He is co-editor of *New Directions in Mathematics Education* and has published several articles on mathematics teaching in books and learned journals.

1 Introduction: At the end of Indulgence

Digby Anderson

1 Allowing children to bring themselves up

'Permissive' has become the word to describe a collection of attitudes to personal morality and child-rearing increasingly dominant in the sixties and early seventies. Inasmuch as one word ever can, it captures many of those attitudes very well: the ethos of non-directiveness, allowing others including children to 'develop' according to their own inclinations, the laudability of autonomy and the perils of being 'judgemental'. Children, left free to develop, to explore and find their own values, their natural innocence uncontaminated by authoritarian intrusion, would blossom into fully developed characters realising their maximum potential.

2 Self-indulgence by husbands and wives

Husbands and wives too were to 'fulfil' themselves. If one stood in the way of the other's fulfilment or if the marriage itself was simply a form masking increasing distance between the partners then it would be best that the form acknowledge the reality and a clean-break be made, an honest, no-fault divorce. This would not harm the children provided one was 'open' about it. Indeed they would be more harmed if the parents tried to keep together a 'hollow-shell' marriage with all its conflicts. Women were encouraged to seek more fulfilling lives by going out to work. Traditional ideas about their roles were out of date and restrictive. Again, provided suitable arrangements were made, no harm would result to the children. They would even profit by the experience their working mother brought back into the home with her from her more fulfilling environment. And in bringing up girls and boys, parents were

9

to be unrestrictive as possible, not encouraging little girls along fixed traditional women's roles.

3 Fads, fashions and experts

'Permissive' does not, cannot cover all the elements of the era. It was also the era of environmentalism. Children would develop more or less regardless of inherited qualities provided the home and school environment was right. It should be warm and supportive. While encouraging them to 'do their own thing', it should not discriminate between them. One did not talk of intelligent and unintelligent children. Oddly, for an age of apparent individualism, difference was played down. Also oddly for an age of autonomy, it was a time of fads and fashions, of conformity in novelty, be it in clothes, music or diet. And it was a culture, again perhaps oddly, of the expert and above all, the counsellor. Parents were to fit in with the fads the experts promoted. And this was especially true of schools where new ways of learning replaced 'old-fashioned' rote lessons.

Towards the end of the era, the coercive elements latent in permissivism came to the fore most obviously in the censorship of books in schools to fit fads of anti-sexism and anti-racism and in teachers requiring parents not to interfere with their new methods by persisting in the old. It was no longer just possible for women to work: they should do so. It was no longer just possible for some girls to learn engineering: no schools should be sexist in their allocation of subjects.

4 The results: crime, self-inflicted disease, poor school achievement, children without fathers

But if permissiveness had become a new orthodoxy, it did not last long. Increasingly discredited by its appalling results in divorce, the number of children brought up without fathers, juvenile crime and poor school achievement, drug abuse and AIDS, it is now in full retreat. At such a time it is only sensible to look once again at its assumptions, the arguments about bringing up children which it supposed were facts.

10

Revaluation has already happened in the political and economic domains. Enterprise, competition and economic responsibility, long pejorative terms, are now, once again, terms of approval. So, to a lesser extent, is patriotism. Matters are less clear in the domain of personal morality and child-rearing. And for good reason.

5 Counter-revolutions more difficult in personal than political matters

It is comparatively easy to change one's political or economic opinions. It costs little. But views about morality and the upbringing of children are tied up with their owners' actual behaviour. People do not just approve of divorce, they divorce. They do not just argue about the way to bring up children, they bring them up. To suggest to many of them that their views are wrong is no mere intellectual challenge: it is to suggest that they may have already damaged their children by their practices over the last two decades.. 'Hush', it is said, 'do not warn of the dangers of one-parent families, even if they are now apparent, for there are now many such families. You will upset them. They have enough trouble without stigma'.

What is more, precisely because child-rearing is about activities not just opinions, it involves skills and habits. Old-fashioned parenthood may have had few theories but it possessed an enormous legacy of traditional habits, skills and wisdom. Re-learning lost wisdoms – if indeed that is what is required – will not come easily.

However there is no choice but at least to consider such wisdoms. The orthodoxy of permissiveness is crumbling and the questions its advocates thought for ever settled in their favour are now, again open for debate. This book revives the controversies they would rather lay undisturbed.

6 The agenda

The matters considered here divide into three interrelated themes. First, what children are and what they need in their upbringing; second, how the behaviour of parents in their relations between each other and in mothers working affect children, third; the impact on parents and children of the fads of teachers, counsellors

11

and 'experts'.

7   The need for discrimination and discipline...

Psychologist, Christopher Brand introduces the first section by stressing the importance of the fact that children differ. Precisely because children differ in their abilities and characters, differences largely explained by genetic factors, it is simply not good enough to provide a generalised background of indiscriminate warmth and encouragement. Rather it is the arduous task of parents to discern the differences in children and provide for them. Moreover, it is also the parents' task to insist that schools, many of which subscribe to a 'comprehensive' ideal which denies differences especially in intelligence and the need for different groupings of different children, recognise their children's varying strengths and weaknesses and make a variety of provisions for them.

Fellow psychologist, Professor Richard Lynn reviews the theory so central to permissiveness that children are naturally good and only corrupted by society. Rather, most psychologists teach that children are inherently – at least partly – savage and need to be taught law-abiding and sociable habits through restraint. Restraint is learned through reward, punishment and example. It is crucial that parents show clear approval for telling the truth, cleanliness, hard work, helpfulness and other virtues, themselves set an example and see that their children's teachers do as well.

8   ...and for the authority, guidance and induction into traditional virtues

It has been fashionable to argue that because we live in an age of change, these virtues are to be discarded in favour of children discovering their own morality. Youth specialist, Errol Mathura points out that technological change in no way reduces the need for teaching 'traditional' moral values. The need for honesty, consideration for others, hard work does not change because we cross the Atlantic by Concorde rather than sail. Nor does the need to inculcate them by habit and with authority. He analyses the fads that have led to the abandonment of authoritative moral and religious teaching in schools and to the cult of the 'non-directive' counsellor. Professor David Marsland agrees. Direction and guidance are not needed only by younger children. Adolescents and young people up to and beyond 21 years of age need adult guidance and the example of role models. Youth is a specific phase of development during which there are special needs and it is during this time that some parents and many 'experts' fail them. Most damage of all has been done by denying this phase of youth exists and pretending that young people are adults. It is essential that parental authority over younger and older children is restored.

9   For the avoidance of fads in nutrition

Fads are also the concern of nutritionist and biologist Dr. Barbara Pickard. Over the last two decades, parents have been besieged by faddists urging them to feed their children more of this or less of that. Exaggerated changes in children's diets – for example, extreme vegetarianism – can carry new and real dangers, she shows. What is needed is the avoidance of extremes, a balanced diet with foods from each of the main groupings and then some tolerance of sweets and crisps as extras. But she also points to the trail of problems left by the decline in parents and children sitting and eating together in a disciplined way.

10   ...and commitment and traditional family structure

Professor Richard Whitfield considers the general question of the needs of children. He argues against sentimentalism and for a love which 'is more a matter of will and commitment than feeling'. It involves judicious giving and witholding and ensures stability through the family structure. The best child development cannot happen if that structure is flawed by separated or absent parents.

11   The damage done by divorce...

Patricia Morgan shows just how damaging separation culminating in divorce can be. Divorce is not better for children than disagreeing parents struggling to keep together. The evidence is that many children regarded their homes prior to divorce, ie during 'conflict' as happy. On divorce they suffer bewilderment, insecurity, rejection and resentment and often continuing conflicts in the subsequent relationships of their parents. The interests of adults and their children do not always coincide. The obligations of parenthood come before the development of 'fulfilled' adult relationships. Parents may well have a duty to stay together 'for the sake of the children'.

12 ...and the need for mothers to be at home with their young children

And women may have an obligation to remain at home. Contemporary society is dismissive or derogatory of women who stay at home to bring up their children. Yet the evidence, argues Lynette Burrows, is that early learning and development of character are crucial to children's overall education and these depend on the continued presence of a mother who provides the necessary love and stimulation.

13 Feminist threats to children at school...

This central role of mothers and hence many women has been subverted by radical feminists who would have girls' schooling more or less ignore it and educate boys and girls regardless of their sex. Dr. Mervyn Hiskett analyses the feminists' arguments and finds them wanting. He urges parents not to be brow-beaten by teachers into abandoning traditional gender distinctions in bringing up their children and to see that the schools do not disregard them either. Such distinctions reflect the reality that for many women, motherhood will indeed be a central part of their life.

14 ...and the effects of abandoning traditional teaching methods

This theme, that parents should beware the fads of experts especially teachers applies not just to ideologies such as feminism but to teaching methods. Dr. Gerry Mulhern explores the example of arithmetic where, in the wake of new teaching methods, as many as seven million people in the UK may be innumerate. At no point were traditional methods such as rote tables shown to be ineffective. They were jettisoned in favour of new ones largely in pursuit of fashion. It was not a fashion suitable for preliterate children. The results have been appalling and comptetence at arithmetic continues to decline. In fact rote learning works well. Children do not find it boring and it does not impair conceptual understanding. Primary schools should get back to basics and ensure that children are numerate.

15   Conclusion: a full circle?

These authors are not recommending a complete return to the prepermissive age. First they only treat a few of the many topics concerned with child-rearing. There has been no room in this collection to consider a host of other topics – the needs of very small children, religious education, the use of television in the home, for example. What is more, if they are read carefully, it will be clear that they do not necessarily agree about all matters. However what their arguments and findings certainly do amount to is a powerful case for a systematic scrutiny of all the ideas and idols of the permissive age in the possibility that child-rearing may indeed need to return part or full circle to the wisdoms which permissiveness sought to replace.

Whatever the conclusions drawn, it is crucial that to the debate on the role of the family, already contributed to by this Unit in *Family Portraits*, there should be added a full and thorough debate on the up-bringing of children. It is to encourage that debate that the Unit publishes these essays.

2 The Changing Advice of Experts on Child-rearing: The Return to Individualism

Christopher Brand

1 Introduction and Summary

Contemporary advice to parents on bringing up children often appears vague, and, precisely because it is vague, inoffensive. Who can quarrel with the exhortations to provide warm and happy homes in which children can develop? But the modern advice *is* tendentious. Its tendentiousness becomes apparent when we contrast it with past models of parenthood. How did uniform, liberal tender-mindedness displace previous conceptions of parenting as an unceasing struggle to improve accents, table manners, dressing skills, tidiness, punctuality and veracity; and to provide special encouragement for the skills of particular, individual children in needlework, horse-riding, boxing and bicycling? When previously was punishment presented as if opposed to love? When, till now, were parents not expected to excite the respect of their children by the distinct good sense and moral authority of their aspirations and plans? In what other age were parents not expected to discern their children's strengths and weaknesses and to cater appropriately for them?

The tendentiousness of modern advice is also clear when we see what the *generalised* ideal of warmth and support does not permit. The very vagueness, the generality of the idea of a good parent is resolutely opposed to the facts: that children differ enormously in their abilities and characters; that these differences are largely explained by genetic differences and by children's own choices of developmental patterns; that different children need to be allowed to choose and create their own milieus in order to develop. The facts emerging from psychological research in the 1980s suggest that parents should be more alert to differences between children in intelligence and character and demand that teachers are too. The important question for parents to ask themselves is not 'Am I providing a sufficiently rich or warm environment?' but 'Am I, in the case of each child, providing options and watching to see how the child uses them?' The same environment, however warm, cannot cater for above and below average IQ children: the former will become bored, the latter frustrated. No amount of extra income or warmth obscures individual differences around which alone real learning seems to take place. The parent's task is not to ignore children's differences by adopting some global ideal of the good home or some global parenting strategy, but to acknowledge and discern difference and provide for it.

Commonsense? For many parents perhaps, but not for many of their advisors who have campaigned long and hard against acknowledging that there are bright and slow children, extrovert and introvert children, careful and careless, funny and solemn children, dextrous and clumsy children, gregarious and solitary children, musical and unmusical children; and who would be horrified at the idea that perhaps there are children with whom mine or yours cannot usefully mix. But the facts, as this review of the history of research shows, point firmly to the central importance of difference. Parents should not struggle to attain some general – or indeed, comprehensive – ideal of 'the good parent' but rather struggle towards that *discretion* and *provision of choice* which alone will allow their children to take the largest strides towards the development of their own individual personalities.

2   Britain's Doctor Spock

Britain's own Doctor Spock was undoubtedly the Scottish solicitor and Waiter to the Signet, George Combe (1788 – 1858). Combe is largely unremembered today; yet for fifty years after his conversion to phrenology in 1820 his name was widely familiar in the drawing rooms of nineteenth century Britain, Ireland and the USA. With the help of a coffee-table visual aid, the phrenological bust, he persuaded the enlightened classes of the nineteenth century to think about characterological virtues as individual possessions that emanated from their brains – and from the brains of their growing children.

A Doctor Spock? Certainly: Combe was the leading British expositor of a Continental theory, phrenology, that he made just as popular as psychoanalysis was to become a century later; and whereas the rituals of psychoanalysis were to offer hope to twentieth century parents only after a substantial financial outlay on therapeutic hours, Combe put his science directly into the hands of the public. Measurement of skull bumps could show what one's child was suited for: exploration, veneration, amativeness, parenting, benevolence and judgment could all be foreseen from a correct appreciation of the skull. Moreover, though Combe himself professed little interest in younger children, believing there was little that could interrupt natural development in the early years, he urged the teaching of phrenology to older children, not least so they should learn 'to what extent they are themselves the arbiters of their own fate'. Combe's *The Constitution of Man*[1] was distributed worldwide – the circulation running to 100,000 copies by 1850. He could lecture virtually anywhere (for example, he gave addresses to packed halls in Glasgow, Newcastle, Frankfurt, Dublin and Pennsylvania) while stipulating that at least 200 people should be present lest phrenology acquire a bad name – a stipulation that no U.K. psychologist apart from Hans Eysenck could make today; and, thanks to the Queen's Consort, Prince Albert, he was asked to advise on the education of the Royal children – an assignment that he accepted eagerly because of his strong belief in the importance of educating children in religious toleration.

Scientific success was to elude Combe. He was soon barred – one has to admit, quite properly – from lecturing on the premises of the University of Edinburgh[2] where, with commendable empiricism, a Professor of Philosophy showed by examination of the human brain at autopsy that there was no correspondence at all between skull bumps and brain bumps. *Phrenology*, as the general (but in 1820 still quite novel) idea that the brain was the seat of the mind, might one day prove acceptable (as it has done in the twentieth century); but *craniology*, the idea that the brain and the mind could be read from skull bumps, was that rare bird, a falsifiable and falsified theory in psychology. Notwithstanding, craniology engaged the sympathies of the talking classes for the next century[3] and its story may serve as something of a Health Warning on the views of today's experts in child development. The chief difference between Mr. Combe and Dr. Spock is that Combe never seriously recanted – as Dr. Spock did in one central matter (admitting that his advice for families in the 1950s and 1960s might have been too liberal and child-centred). In this difference it is Combe who must seem a more mainstream figure in the ranks of popular psychology.

3 The trend to liberal child-rearing: the neglect of individual differences between children

Advice by experts in child-rearing has changed since Combe's day. Today it is – we can safely assume – better informed by empirical medical knowledge and it is now more liberal, at least in the senses of aiming to appear less restrictive of both parents and children and of being even less moralistic and less traditional than Combe's. Today's advice is more conspicuously concerned to nurture what may pass for affection – usually assuming that the positive bond of sentiment between parent and child is of central concern and is to be preserved at all costs. Finally, it is more egalitarian (or similitarian[4]) both in its general reluctance to admit that there are lasting differences between children; and in its approval of the prevailing communal ethic that children should receive their education in mixed-ability groupings of their age peers from the nursery onwards until tertiary education is begun.

Gone are the weekly purges, the blood-lettings, the cure-all potions made from pigeons' entrails and the powdered skulls of Egyptian mummies, the advice to keep children's arms in splints to prevent masturbation, and – very largely – the Sunday gathering of the family to attend divine worship or to read the scriptures. Such arrangements are no longer favoured. In their place we find useful advice about colic, nightmares and travel-sickness; a disdain for punishment that may prove shareable enough in the better-off home with its wider variety of bribes and inducements; a concern to preserve supposedly fragile human relationships[5] rather than to use these relationships urgently to bring swift progress by the child towards what used to be called socialisation; and a preference that children should be exposed as early as possible to diets free of lead, sugar, salt, milk and protein, and to teaching purged of racism, sexism, elitism, neo-colonialism and heterosexism.[6] Gone is the Scottish Mama who boasted 'My children love me and fear me as sinners dread death'.[7] Gone is the hierarchial American Frontier family of around 1820 where 'not much affection was exchanged between its members, as affection was thought to undermine obedience and destroy authority'.[8] Gone too is John Stuart Mill's education (at his father's hands) 'not of love but of fear'.

4   The involvement of official psychologists in the latest advice

Surprisingly or not, this package of changes cannot be traced to the influence of any one real expert in child psychology, nor indeed to any particular school of psychological thought. George Combe, for example, was a champion of liberalism and affection; but not of any medical empiricism that would distract from his main concern for the development of the whole personality;[9] nor of any sameness or utopianism of treatment that his ideas of brain-based individuality led him to oppose. Combe was quick to observe that Robert Owen's pioneering social environmentalism in New Lanark 'did not make sufficient allowance for the development of individual character.' By contrast, the arch-behaviourist, B.F. Skinner,[10] whose ideas so appealed to twentieth-century intellectuals around the low point of hereditarian and eugenic thought in 1945, was in favour of conspicuous affection – at least ruling out punishment as inefficacious for children, just as he found it to be for rats and pigeons – and of that similitude of treatment which the laws of learning seemed to decree; but he was not at all sympathetic to 'the medical model' nor to any form of liberalism that would free children (or indeed adults) from proper attempts by experts to 'shape' their behaviour. John Bowlby,[11] for long the best known British child psychoanalyst, stressed the importance of affection but not of liberalism: for he abhorred what he took to be the disastrous consequences of family break-up and maternal deprivation, and even seemed to caution against 'working mothers' (in days before Women's Lib had arrived on the scene). The influential American psychologist and educator, Jerome Bruner[12] probably comes nearest to sympathising with all the four changes in advice to parents; but even he has seemed to doubt the importance of medical and biological knowledge – conspicuously declining to suppose that human psychological development derives in any interesting way from the infrastructural, physical features of our genes and nervous systems.

How then do we come by the prototype of well-advised parenting that modern 'baby and child care' writers have in mind? The advisers' prototype (as displayed in the popular books of Penelope Leach and Bruno Bettelheim[13]) is essentially of a non-idiosyncratic, rational mother who might almost dote on her child were there not a need to preserve her own sanity and of course, her career; and who, while she may master some of the skills of the nurse and the primary schoolteacher, is not markedly concerned to lead her child in any particular direction – and certainly not at the expense of the good and enjoyable relationship that is the only valid reason for venturing upon parenthood in the first place. How did uniform, liberal idealism; (with a little medical realism thrown in) arrive on the scene and displace previous conceptions of parenting as an unceasing struggle to improve accents, table-manners, dressing skills, tidiness, punctuality, veracity and the use of the handkerchief in most children; and to provide special encouragement for the drawing, swimming, bicycling, recitatory, violining, boxing or animal-husbandry skills of some of them?

The prime mover in these changes is in fact not hard to find. In many ways the last century in the West has seen a decline in *philosophical* individualism – a decline in belief in the importance, and even in the very existence, of individual personality. Our intellectuals have moved us away from an understanding of society as made up of individuals having enduring attributes, the origins of which attributes were once either simply mysterious or otherwise traceable (*via* family likenesses) to biological factors and to early moral training. Despite an enormous increase in *behavioural* individualism, and indeed in deviance and criminality, we have all been pushed by social scientific theorists towards an understanding of people as malleable by society and thus only temporarily different – 'temporarily' often meaning, of course, 'until that great day of social revolution when niggardliness in welfare spending will be relegated to the past and when the ratio of experts in caring to cases of social disadvantage will be one-to-one.' In adumbration of this new understanding, social psychologists in the West have spent much of the past twenty years arguing (in their learned journals, and with the help of countless statistics on psychology sophomores) whether people have enduring personalities at all.[14]

According to Russian and American psychologists of sixty years ago, we might all be changed by the methods of conditioning.[15] Today the traditional 'laws of learning' in psychology are not even considered adequate to explaining most of the behaviour of the house mouse (the main skills of which are now known to be largely innate); yet many social psychologists insist on tracing the personality differences of mankind to 'situations' (long after the repeated use of that word in the Watergate hearings made it a by-word for evasiveness and mendacity), to stereotypes, to 'labels' to self-delusion, or to anything (often called 'complex interaction effects') that would spare them acknowledging individual people as real, irreducible and active agents on the social scene. It may be that, because of the enormous increase in geographical mobility in the West, psychological researchers of today seldom have the experience of meeting schoolmates with whom they grew up. Perhaps they are deprived of that kind of re-encounter – not without its embarrassing aspects – in which one person is moved to say of an old friend (now perhaps in a very different social bracket and having experienced several changes of spouse, geographical location, job title and political affiliation) 'You haven't changed a bit![16] Alternatively, it may be that some more considered motivation induces denial of human realities that are inconvenient for egalitarians.

At least one such motivation of anti-individualistic theorists is sometimes voiced quite publicly: their fear is that any substantial acknowledgement of the constitutional bases of human personality will, in its 'determinism', lead to social pessimism, to a decline in reforming zeal, and to restricted prospects of State employment for those who profess expertise (especially of a 'social' rather than of a medical kind) in how, to change people for the better.

However anti-individualism itself comes about, it is most probably from this deep moral change in our understanding of human personhood that we arrive at the 'empty parent' and 'empty child' prototypes of the modern baby-look. For, since individuality is considered unreal, or at least readily changeable, it need not be catered for. Thus there is no need to advise, say, religious parents (or, equally, irreligious parents) on how to raise their child so that it will eventually share their own beliefs and outlook; nor any advice on how to elicit the best from a child who is, in the very long haul, frankly an extrovert. At the same time, avoidance of the topic of individuality helps the experts out of explaining why children do often depart markedly from parental ideals and models; and out of considering what most parents know soon after the arrival of their second child, that marked differences occur between siblings (sharing only 50 per cent of their genes as they do) even when they have been handled in a very similar way.

Perhaps the 'empty parent' side of the coin may not seem such a bad idea for a saleable book of improving advice. Perhaps, in a tolerant, multi-cultured, multi-ethnic society, one can hardly expect the experts to be found advising parents on the achievement of idiosyncratic objectives. Yet the anti-individualistic prototype of the 'empty child' – or at least of the child whose own individuality is invariably considered to be of a short-term nature, as the presently irritable, shy or independent-minded child 'goes through' what is suggested hopefully to be a mere 'phase' of development – is a very serious matter. For it flies in the face of hard-won truths about child development as they have appeared to psychological researchers in recent years.

5 Modern developmental research: accounting for difference

There are two main sources of factual knowledge about child development. One is the psychogenetic approach which uses twin-studies and adoption-studies to inquire what causes children to differ – especially tracing measured variation to long-term influences of children's differences in genetic make-up and family background. The other is the Piagetian approach which endeavours to describe the developmental routes taken by children – possibly by individual children, but more commonly, in most Piagetian research, by the average child.

It often appears that these two research traditions, of the

psychogeneticist and the Piagetian, are at odds with each other. The psychogeneticist talks primarily about the relative influence of genetic differences as opposed to environmental differences in the final production of measured variety; while the Piagetian talks about the interplay of these influences along the developmental route as biological changes in the growing child produce, in conjunction with, say, a propitious environment, a series of leaps forward over time into greater intelligence and maturity. The appearance of conflict is heightened by the reluctance of the two camps to speak each other's language, to use each other's methods, and to recognize that children's abilities as measured by 'old-fashioned' IQ tests (of vocabulary, reasoning and memory) invariably correlate highly with their abilities as measured by 'new-fangled' Piagetian tests of 'conservation', 'perspective taking' and 'formal cperations'.

Nevertheless, the fact is that Piaget's followers seldom go into print opposing the regular empirical claims of psychogenetic researchers that, when measured at some one point in time, children's enormous differences in mental ability and personality are substantially heritable – genetic variation accounting for somewhere around 50 per cent of measured psychological differences between children according to modern studies.[17] Rather, the reaction of Piagetians to marked similarities between separated identical twins and to marked dissimilarities between adopted children reared together is one of boredom – apparently because such findings tell us so little in detail about how, precisely, individual differences come about. Maybe some children do indeed have superior 'genes for' intelligence or self-control or affection; yet, Piagetians will say, such genes did not create these children's test scores without some massive interplay with the environment which, if only it were understood, would allow dramatic remediation for those children whose interactions with the environment had not yielded such happy results in the sad human condition of pre-revolutionary days.

The psychogeneticist too, experiences boredom rather than outright hostility as he considers the Piagetian scene. Of course children with a genetic advantage for IQ 'interact' more successfully with their environments – building up their finally measured intelligence by such techniques as reading faster, thus amassing a richer informational base, and then using that extra knowledge and confidence to widen their reading and to move on to solve new problems that they previously avoided. Thus, indeed, do genes play out, via the child's exploration and utilization of its environment into final measured abilities on diverse tests. Yet psychogeneticists do not detect any specific scientific interest of such entirely likely processes while Piagetians provide few testable hypotheses as to the exact nature of such interactions of growing children with their environments – and certainly not while these interactions are thought by their inchoate champions to provide some kind of alternative to admitting the importance of genetic factors.

In this pseudo-contest, it is the psychogeneticist who has had more of a shock in recent years. The shock has been that while estimates of the genetic contribution to intelligence have declined somewhat, estimates of the importance of external, environmental features have not risen correspondingly. Jensen[18] and Eysenck[19] used to estimate that intelligence was around 75 per cent heritable; at the same time they committed themselves to a modest environmentalist claim that the social class of a child's parents and the degree of non-class-related enrichment in the home (the variation arising, for example, from differences in nutrition, parental warmth and socialization procedures) had small but definite effects accounting for some 15 per cent of eventual differences in intelligence; and the remaining 10 per cent of IQ variance was attributable to measurement error. Today, estimates of IQ's heritability have moved lower – to around 60 per cent, or even 50 per cent in some studies that have arguably involved too few children at the extremes of the IQ distribution; yet there is no reason from modern studies to assign any more effect to the child's family environment than Jensen and Eysenck originally calculated. – An important adoption study conducted in France makes this pretty clear:[20] in this study (directed by the former nuclear physicist, Maurice Schiff) each standard deviation[21] of parental social class was worth only the 3.35 IQ points to children that Jensen and Eysenck had long hypothesized. So the question arises for the psychogeneticist: what is to fill the gap as traditionally conceived genetic and environmental influences prove, between them, insufficient to account for all the variance?

Psychogeneticists, it may be remarked, are actually shockable: for they are committed to accounting for 100 per cent of the variance somehow, whether by the various genetic influences-of breeding, of assortative mating by parents (like marrying like), and of gene-gene interactions that will make genetically identical people especially similar; whether by the influence of the environment; whether by genetic-environmental correlation – if the 'best' genes occur in association with the 'best' environments; or whether by specifiable interaction effects – producing for example good violining skills only when *both* genes and environment are propitious. Any observation that these influences do not add up to 100 per cent of observed trait variance is an embarrassment. By contrast, it is seldom clear what could ever embarrass Piagetians – unless it might possibly be the sheer range of doubts concerning the most traditional and originally inspiring Piagetian claims.[22] Yet these doubts, as to whether there are any marked 'stages' of development, have only added to the obscurity and unfalsifiability of Piagetianism: for they have required a deep retreat by Piagetians into the vagueness of talk about the complex intricacies of development that do not lend themselves to general theoretical formulations. Lately there has been considerable agreement amongst Piagetians themselves that their former fascination for describing young children as 'egocentric' was a mistake.[23] Yet further research into this non-phenomenon is still deemed by Piagetian gurus to be in order even though there is very little to study and not even a half-adequate theory to guide further expenditures of Piagetian time and taxpayers' monies.

However that may be, can psychogeneticists actually handle their own problem of the failure of detectable genetic and environmental influences (together with their co-variance and statistical interaction) to account for the final variety in children's abilities and personalities? Lately it has appeared that they can, and that there are exciting new concepts, methods and findings that may soon draw many developmental psychologists into a recognition of broad agreement. Four observations are particularly interesting, as follows.

6 Children develop by choosing their own environments

In Sandra Scarr's work with identical (or monozygotic (MZ)) and fraternal (or dizygotic (DZ)) twins[24] it was discovered that similarities in intelligence amongst MZs were particularly striking – as compared to the similarities amongst DZs – only when the twins reached adolescence. Earlier, at around the age of seven, the MZ-DZ difference in similarity was slight in this work, with twins resembling each other almost regardless of their degree of genetic similarity. Yet, over time, the MZ twins appeared to stay similar to each other while the DZ twins became less similar, with the final consequence that intelligence appears more heritable in adolescence than it is in childhood. The most convincing explanation of this finding, Scarr suggests, is that, as the twins have more opportunity to select and create their own environments, the DZ twins (who are no more genetically similar than are siblings) make different choices, while the MZ twins (who are genetically identical) make similar choices. Arguably, as one DZ twin prefers Shakespeare to soap-opera, or quiet friends to noisy ones, the DZ twins' own chosen environments (perhaps best called *milieus*) feed back to cause further differences between them.

Here, perhaps, Scarr's research method is allowing us to see what might be called a process of *transaction* (to distinguish it from the numerous possible uses of the term 'interaction' that have made for confusion in the past). The *transaction* is that Genotype –> Phenotype$_1$ (ie, what the child is actually like at some earlier stage, 'Time 1') –> Milieu –> Phenotype$_2$ Here we are dealing not with an environmental influence from the outside, from the child's school or parents, but with a milieu that the child has chosen for itself, perhaps partly in anticipation of what it could cope with. The child selects to have violin instruction rather than to watch TV; and its violining skills then improve. At the same time there is also a fully external environmental variable that may be at work to modify such transaction: for there will always be the question of what choices the external environment actually allows the child to make. In general, it seems reasonable to suppose that the adolescent in the modern West has more opportunity for choice than the seven-year old; but the scope may still be larger for some children than for

27

others even though quite a wide range of options is made generally available (in all but the most educated homes today) by the buttons on the TV set.

7   Parents can help to bring to fruition differences which already exist

In a major scholarly follow-up to these ideas, Plomin and Daniels[25] have provided evidence from their Colorado Adoption Project that adoptive children who grow up in the same family show little similarity to each other in personality at any age – and not even much similarity in intelligence once they are adolescent. Although few of these adoptees experienced especially harsh conditions of rearing – ie their range of social environments was somewhat restricted, few of them growing up in especially poor homes – Plomin and Daniels' finding is still a blow to most of those conventional forms of environmentalist thought that assume differences between families to be importantly causal to personality development. At the same time, however, Plomin and Daniels remark the quite modest correlations (of around 0.50 for personality traits) that obtain even between MZ twins who grow up together sharing both genes and environment as fully as possible. Thus they conclude that, beyond the substantial genetic influences on development, there may be rather few straightforward influences of the family upon its children in general; instead, there are marked *within-*family environmental effects whereby families generate marked differences *between* growing children, perhaps as a response to initially slight phenotypic differences.

Apparently, the family 'environment' is important not in creating differences that distinguish children in one family from those in another, but in bringing to a larger fruition those detectable differences that already exist (genotypically or phenotypically) between children in the same family. What is causal, surprisingly, is not any general parental influence (applied as this would be to all the children equally, and yielding as it does virtually no detectable effect on adoptees), but rather the individuated parental response to particular children that results in further difference between them. Apparently, a parent's being a bank manager will give its children no more of a general tendency to thrift, book-keeping ability, or whatever, than is given by such 'bank manager genes' as have been passed on; but all parents are able, by judicious response to their individual children, to help some of them by environmental means to be more like bank-managers than others. One way in which such genetic and within-family pressures work might be that, like a team, a family from time to time has various role-vacancies – for a family extrovert and humourist, for someone who is interested in gadgets and their repair, for a diplomat, for a nurse, for a person who tidies up, for a realist, an idealist and so on. Perhaps children move to fill these vacancies when parents and siblings have not already done so, and thus each family ends with quite a wide spread of personality types. Again, there may be rebound effects within the family: it is sometimes said that a pessimist is someone who has grown up with an optimist. Yet, whatever the processes that generate within-family differences, some of them building directly on children's inherited proclivities, others being of entirely social origin, the absence of any general environmental effect of families on their children is striking.

8 Particular children may require particular environments

Sadly, much British developmental work today assumes rather than puts to the test the influence of social-environmental factors. But mere empirical correlations, so long as they are collected, sometimes set bells ringing unexpectedly. Thus Joan Freeman[26] found when comparing 'gifted' children (of above IQ 140) with children who are merely 'bright' (around IQ 120), that the quality of the home environment correlates much more strongly with child IQ in the case of the former, gifted children than in the case of the latter. Again, this result may make some sense if children are seen primarily as seeking environmental opportunities for expression. Apparently, many homes today provide quite sufficient options for ordinarily bright children, and the considerable differences between such homes are not of detectable consequence to child IQ; but, once a child is of superior intelligence, some home environments are markedly limiting on further development, while others can respond to and in turn stimulate mental growth, leading to the

29

observed child-environment correlation amongst gifted children.

9 Children's biology influences the use they can make of their environment

The latest report of the mysteries and limits of the supposedly potent external environment involves a novel analysis of Colorado Adoption Project data by Bergeman and Plomin.[27] Here it turns out that while children who grow up in their own biological families show a modest correlation of .37 between their own intellectual level and measures of the relative enrichment versus deprivation of their home circumstances, adopted children growing up in a similar range of families show no such correlation. Apparently the correlation that appears in biological families cannot be given its most obvious environmentalist interpretation – that enriched home environments boost IQ a little. Rather, biological features (of parent-child similarity for genetic reasons) seem to influence whether a child is able to use and adapt to the type of environment that its parents supply. Once again, we seem to have to envisage some active process of transaction whereby children's biology influences what they can extract from and relate to in their home environments.

10 The crucial question: can the child effect change in its environment according to its own developing personality and abilities?

In short, the thrust of new research in developmental psychology is as follows. First, genetic differences are the main identifiable causes of the marked psychological differences that distinguish children of the same chronological age. (This conclusion is not seriously contested by developmental researchers, though Piagetian theorists still prefer to dismiss it as somehow uninteresting.)

Secondly, some 40 years of enthusiasm for environmentalist possibilities have not yielded any major discovery of social treatments or practices that have a substantial general impact on child intelligence or personality. Even raising the socio-economic level of a child's home by four standard deviations (virtually the entire range of class differences in the general population) would only be worth about 14 IQ points to the child on culture-reduced IQ tests;[28] and efforts to develop Headstart-type programmes have disclosed no previously unremarked sources of substantial variation.[29] Differences in provision by adults that distinguish one family from another and one pre-educational programme from another are, quite simply, amazingly uninfluential on children. As David Hay put it in his recent textbook,[30] 'In practical terms we have a situation where parents exert [environmentally] no general effects over personality development in their children'.

Thirdly, there is increasing recognition that the child's individual biological make-up and completed phenotype at any one stage are important influences on its transactions with the environment, admitting creation and selection of *milieu* in so far as opportunities allow. Children constantly make choices if they can. The question about their environments is not as to whether they are globally 'good' or 'bad', for such a question can apparently have little meaning. Rather, the crucial question is: Can the child effect change in its environment according to its own developing personality and abilities? In nature, apparently, personality development is not a matter of the environment influencing personality but of personality acting – when this is possible – to select and shape the environment.

11   The bottom line: cater for individuality

Little of this growing, empirically based consensus as to the existence and causal importance of biologically given individuality and its transactive working out is indicated to parents today. Piagetians must take some responsibility here. For, as their own hopes of becoming a dominant force in child psychology and education receded because of lack of conspicuous attainment, they settled in their own studies for increasingly banal work in their own tradition that might just realize the egalitarian pieties of many of them; they continued to hope that children differed chiefly in their 'stages' of development and that no long-term distinctions between children needed to be recognized; they counselled against special education[31] – and thus in effect against any education – for brighter children who were to be judged according to their chronological ages as unsuitable for exposure to, for example, symbolic thought; and they obfuscated the importance of children's biological natures rather than admit openly the convergence of their own main results with the findings deriving from trait psychology and psychogenetics. Yet the end of this gloomy and unproductive period for Piagetians is now in sight as more conventional approaches of greater scientific rigour have begun to show them how to explore the very 'interaction effects' of which they were so long but so vaguely enamoured.

How can parents respond to an appreciation that – whatever the current child care books may intone as they venerate egalitarian and similitarian aspirations – modern research is fully supportive of the need to recognise and to cater for individuality? There are possibly many improvements that parents could make – for their own children and for the children of others: by being more alert to differences; by having their children professionally tested; by encouraging schools to provide realistic assessments; by standing up for the traditional family[32] – within which children can truly become known, unlike in the more anonymous arrangements so favoured by reformers; by realizing that not all attempts at description can be dismissed as 'labelling'; and by opposing generalist curricula in schools that hold children back from real proficiency at any subject until they are in their twenties. No-one can be certain that such an ideological shift would be decisively utopian: for the fact is that individuality has in any case persisted as a major force in child development even under the most determined twentieth-century attempts to deny its influence and even to stamp it out. Yet it seems obvious that parental attempts at improvement will be more effective if they accord with the ways in which development and change occur in nature; and there is no point in pursuing heroic undifferentiated programmes of socialisation and education against which nature has pretty clearly set its face.

What must be emphasised is this. There is no reliable way of seriously limiting a child's mental development by modest (say one standard deviation below par) failures of stimulation or encouragement. Even such a grave loss as that of a parent, harrowing as it is to a child in the short term, is compensatable and has few detectable adverse effects by adulthood: indeed, serious parental deprivation (normally by the early death of one or both parents) has been the lot of some 40 per cent of American Presidents, British Prime Ministers, and first-rank Western philosophers.[33]

By contrast, it is certainly arguable that lack of choice and lack of opportunity must sometimes be a serious hazard: this must be the implication of the apparent involvement of transaction effects that seem to be so largely at work in normal development according to modern research. If options are important in allowing genetic expression, the cardinal thought that the modern parent should cultivate is not 'Am I providing a sufficiently 'rich' environment?' but, much more particularly, 'Am I providing options and watching the results?' Arguably, if more parents asked themselves 'What is the child's serious alternative to sitting in front of the TV?' or even 'What is the serious alternative, which I would encourage equally, to helping with the washing-up?' a more satisfactory ethos of child-rearing would be created, involving the use of parental intelligence, determination, creativity, application and sensitivity rather than the crude and largely unavailing use of cash resources.[34]

Naturally, faced with a world of choices, some children will make the 'wrong' choices, as they have doubtless done in the past. But it is precisely at this point that the individuality of the parent can be allowed to re-intrude upon the scene. So long as parents allow a number of options at any point and monitor how they are taken up there is good reason for parents to exercise their own discretion – partly considering what is known of the child's individual propensities, of course – as to what the range of options should be. This, at least, is the path to genuine child development that nature conspicuously provides.

For parents to ask themselves repeatedly 'What am I allowing this child to choose right now?' will prove a startling exercise even within the middle-class home. But asking it will most often yield the answer 'Nothing' when the question is asked of a child's typical day at a British State-run primary school. In these schools our children now languish for years with little possibility of escaping the enforced egalitarian company of their ill-assorted age peers of all ability levels. Whatever choice of *milieu* children have at home is snatched away as they enter the school gates and are treated chiefly according to their chronological, rather than according to their mental age. As a result, many higher-IQ children become bored and listless; and many lower-IQ children are frustrated by endless defeat when even the simple-minded 'education' that is provided – commonly rehearsing what has already been absorbed by their brighter age-peers from parents and TV – proves beyond their own capacities. After practising at home the exercise of asking 'What are my child's options?' the modern parent will, it is hoped, be found moving out into the wider world with sensible versions of that same question for the educators of today.

In fact, the parent who urges choice will find a warm reception from many a practised schoolteacher: for although the official piety of educational authorities, as of child care experts, is egalitarian, experienced teachers have typically set behind them the bizarre preachments of Piagetians and Marxists whom they encountered at teacher-training college, and the obsession of these archaic pundits with social class.[35] At home, children need parents to focus their efforts not on pointless attempts to be a 'better parent' on some simple scale of affluence or enlightenment but on the exercise of enabling individual children to enjoy the exploration of options that parents' sensitive discretion has provided. In their dealings with schools, the parents' task is even simpler: here the child has nothing to lose from empirically-informed individualism unless it be the strange and unwanted shackles of State-imposed similitarianism. In such reasonable efforts, parents at last have the experts increasingly behind them. At least, as Plomin and Daniels put it:

> If the effects of parents on children lie in the unique environ-ments they provide for each child [rather than in what parents provide for *all* their children], childrearing books need to be rewritten, and early childhood education and interventions aimed at the prevention of psychopathology need to be rethought.[36]

Notes and References

1. G. Combe, *A System of Phrenology*, 5th edtn., Maclachlan and Stewart, 1853.
2. Nothing daunted, Combe continued to lecture to the university students who flocked to hear him in the George Street Assembly Rooms – nowadays best known as the major

venue for the Edinburgh Festival Fringe.

3. Britain's most famous psychologist of all time, Sir Francis Galton, began his scientific career, initially as an anthropologist and geographer in South West Africa, partly in response to a skull reading that indicated his capacity for adventure.

4. Modern egalitarianism in the West goes much further than the demand for equality of opportunity, and further even than Lenin's relatively modest insistence on equality of social position: for Lenin thought it 'quite obvious that men are unequal in their abilities' and claimed that 'no socialist ever forgot this'.

5. Even romps in bed between parents and children were encouraged in one book that appeared before the anxieties of the mid-1980s about father-daughter incest.

6. Class-ist teaching is still tolerated however: it is apparently permissible to teach middle-class children to have a social conscience about their origins.

7. H.G. Graham, *The Social Life of Scotland in the Eighteenth Century*, A & C Black, 1899.

8. Frances Fitzgerald, *Cities on a Hill: Journeys through Contemporary American Cultures*, Simon and Schuster, 1986.

9. Combe doubted the usefulness of exploring the brain's functions by observing the results of surgery. He cites with approval a writer who deplored the brain being 'so mechanically cut down upon...as to constitute a sort of exhibition connected with nothing'.

10. B.F. Skinner, *Walden Two*, Macmillan, New York, 1948; and *Upon Further Reflection*, Prentice Hall, 1987.

11. J.S. Bowlby, *International Journal of Psychoanalysis*, Vol. 39, 1958, pp. 350–373.

12. J.S. Brunner, *The Process of Education*, Harvard University Press, 1961; and *Actual Minds, Possible Worlds*, Harvard University Press, 1986.

13. B. Bettelheim, *A Good Enough Parent: the Guide to Bringing Up Your Child*, Thames and Hudson, 1987; Penelope Leach, *Baby and Child*, Penguin, 1977.

14. D.J. Bem and A. Allen, *Psychological Review*, Vol. 81, no. 6, 1974, pp. 506–520; A. Furnham and J. Jaspars, *Personality and Individual Differences*, Vol. 6, No. 4, 1985, pp. 513–514; D.T. Kenrick and D.O. Stringfield, *Psychological Review* Vol. 87, no. 1, 1980, pp. 88–104; W. Mischel, *Personality and Assessment*, Wiley, 1968.

15. These doctrines doubtless reflected the enthusiasm that affected even hard-headed behaviourist psychologists such as the Russians and Americans of the 1920s bent themselves to building great new nation-states out of disparate human material across unprecedented geographical distances.

16. Anti-individualist theorists typically deny even the existence of lasting IQ differences. In fact a recent study found a correlation of .78 for IQ over 40 years amongst some 250 Canadian army recruits of the 1940s: A.E. Schwartzman, Dolores Gold, D. Andres, T.Y. Arbuckle and June Chaikelson, *Canadian Journal of Psychology*, Vol. 41, no. 2, 1987, pp. 244–256.

17. Constance Holden, *Science*, Vol. 237, 1987, pp. 598–601; R. Plomin and Denise Daniels, *The Behavioural and Brain Sciences*, Vol. 10, 1987, pp. 1–60.

18. A.R. Jensen, *Genetics and Education*, Methuen, 1972.

19. H.J. Eysenck, *The Structure and Measurement of Intelligence*, Medical & Technical Press, 1979.

20. C.R. Brand, *Nature*, Vol. 325, 1987, p. 767.

21. The unit of divergence from the mean – where four standard deviations embrace the variation shown in both directions by 95 per cent of the population.

22. C.J. Brainerd, *The Behavioural and Brain Sciences*, Vol. 1, no. 2, 1978, pp. 350–373; C.R. Brand, 'What can a Piagetian assimilate?', *Psychology News*, Vol. 1, no. 38, 1985, pp. 14–15.

23. C.R. Brand, 'Egocentric children – or eccentric psychologists?' *Psychology News*, Vol. 2, no. 2, 1988, pp. 19–21.

24. Sandra Scarr and K. McCartney, *Child Development*, Vol. 54, 1983, pp. 424–435.

25. *The Behavioural and Brain Sciences*, op. cit.
26. Joan Freeman, 'Gifted children', in C.J. Turner and H.B. Miles (eds.), *The Biology of Intelligence*, Nafferton Books, 1984.
27. C.S. Bergeman and R. Plomin, 'Parental mediators of the genetic relationship between home environment and infant mental development', *British Journal of Developmental Psychology*, Vol. 6, no. 1, 1988, pp. 11–19.
28. *Nature*, Vol. 325, op. cit.
29. H.H. Spitz, *The Raising of Intelligence: A Selected History of Attempts to Raise Retarded Intelligence*, Lawrence Erlbaum Associates, 1986.
30. D.A. Hay, *Essentials of Behavioural Genetics*, Blackwell, 1985.
31. Margaret Donaldson, *Children's Minds*, Croom Helm, 1978.
32. The adoption of such a pro-family position will be that much easier for readers of two recent important defences of the family: B. Berger and P.L. Berger, *The War over the Family*, Hutchinson, 1983; F. Mount, *The Subversive Family: An Alternative History of Love and Marriage*, 1982.
33. B–A. Scharfstein, *The Philosophers*, Blackwell, 1980.
34. Needless to say one of the few environmental influences making for intellectual growth in children is that of the intellectual level of the parents and siblings who surround them: R.B. Zajonc, *Psychological Bulletin*, Vol. 93, no. 3, 1983, pp. 457–480.
35. For an exhortation as to the forthcoming 'end of classism' see editorial in *Biology and Society*, Vol. 4, no. 3, 1987.
36. *Behavioural and Brain Sciences*, op. cit.

3 On the Necessity of Teaching Children Moral Restraint

Richard Lynn

1 Summary and Introduction

The popular, romantic theory of childhood holds that children are inherently good and corrupted only by society. Most psychologists teach the opposite. Children are inherently – at least partly – savage and need to learn law-abiding and sociable habits through restraint. Restraint operates through reward and punishment which are later internalised in conscience. It is crucial that parents should express clear approval for telling the truth, cleanliness, work, helpfulness etc. and equally clear disapproval of their opposites. Children also learn by modelling themselves on their parents and therefore it is necessary for parents to set good examples. Schools need to teach both by rewards and punishments and by providing models, but current trends to egalitarianism have devalued achievement, example and competition.

Some children grow up to be unsuccessful, unsociable or criminal because of factors beyond the control of parents and school: ability to learn is influenced by heredity. But in other cases the remedies lie with the parents and schools who need to take a realistic view of children's wayward propensities and teach clear and firm standards through example and discipline.

2 Socialisation: developing children's self-control over anti-social propensities

Throughout the ages parents have faced the problem of transforming their children from wild little savages into morally aware, law-abiding and socially responsible adults. This is the problem of socialisation.

There are two broad schools of thought about the nature of socialisation. The first is embodied in the Christian doctrine of original sin. It holds that children are innately disposed to selfishness and evil, and that measures of various kinds have to be taken by parents, teachers and others to develop the child's self control over anti-social propensities. This is the view of all the leading contemporary psychologists who have made serious analyses of this question.

The alternative view, sometimes called the romantic theory of the nature of children, received its classical statement in 1762 in Jean Jacques Rousseau's *Emile*. It holds that children are naturally good and only rendered selfish and anti-social by the corrupting influences of society. This view has made a good deal of headway in the present century among informed public opinion and has been a factor in the relaxation of discipline, the growth of the permissive society and the weakening of the belief in punishment for the wrong-doing of children and adult criminals. It has become widely accepted among educationists and has been an element in the reduction of the role of competition in schools, which many educationists view as a coercive device to encourage undesirable striving for personal achievement. Nevertheless, in spite of these trends in the *zeitgeist* of the present century, leading contemporary psychological theory on socialisation adheres much more closely to the older conception of original sin.

3 Sigmund Freud: advocate of restraint

In the debate on the socialisation process there has been no more misunderstood figure than Sigmund Freud. In the popular mind Freud is identified with the view that inhibition causes neurosis and that therefore children should be brought up free of inhibition and restraint. Freud's actual theories on child-development were quite the contrary and belong essentially with the original sin school of thought.

Freud held that young children are dominated by the Id, the seat of selfish and unrestrained sexual and aggressive instincts. It is the task of parents and society to develop the Super-ego, an internal control mechanism to restrain the Id impulses either by inhibition or by redirection, through sublimation, into socially acceptable and worthwhile activities. Normally by the time the child is six years old this repression has been satisfactorily accomplished and the Super-ego has been formed. The children then enter the so called latency period which lasts for some six years. During this time the energies of the Id are directed through sublimation into the acquisition of knowledge. Sublimation continues throughout life, to different degrees among different individuals. Freud wrote a study of Leonardo da Vinci, in whom he maintained that sublimation was very effective and that this was the source of Leonardo's prolific scientific and artistic achievements. More generally, Freud maintained in *Civilisation and Its Discontents* that the effective repression of natural anti-social instincts, particularly unrestrained sexuality and aggression, are an essential precondition for civilisation.

Freud's views were therefore very different from those with which he is popularly credited. Far from believing that children should be brought up unrestrained, he maintained that the development of internal restraints is essential and that if parents and society failed in this process, civilisation would collapse.

4   The moral development of children

The leading contemporary work on the development of moral values in children has been done by Lawrence Kohlberg.[1] He has concluded that children pass through several stages of moral development. In the first stage young children understand the concepts of right and wrong solely in terms of the physical consequences to themselves. An action is perceived as wrong if the parents disapprove and the child receives punishment for it. At this stage they are not naturally good but behave well by virtue of the anticipated consequences of their parents' disapproval and punishment.

Older children and adolescents come to formulate general principles of right and wrong in terms of what is beneficial to society as a whole. Their moral codes have become internalised, their conscience has developed and restrains them from wrong-doing. In addition, they are still aware that many kinds of wrong-doing are criminal offences and subject to punishment. Hence by the time they are adolescents the great majority of young people behave in socially acceptable ways through two distinct psychological mechanisms. Firstly, they retain the awareness of the potentiality of punishment. Secondly, they have developed an internalised moral code, experienced as conscience, which is perceived as a set of moral principles to which they should adhere.

Neither of these mechanisms of moral restraint is inborn in children. Some children fail to learn these moral restraints and these develop into habitual criminals and psychopaths. Moral restraint has to be learned and it is learned principally in the family from parents.

5   The conditioning theory of socialisation

A good deal of attention has been given to the processes through which children come to learn moral restraint. It is now generally considered that two processes operate. The first is conditioning. The leading exponent of this theory is H.J. Eysenck.[2] According to this theory parents show approval to their children for a wide range of socialised behaviours such as telling the truth, consideration for others, helpfulness, cleanliness, doing well at school and so forth. They also express disapproval for an equally wide range of unsocialised behaviours, such as telling lies, selfishness, dirtiness, physical aggression, inappropriate sexual behaviour and conversation, doing poorly at school and so on.

The expression of approval and disapproval of socialised and unsocialised behaviour is an important part of the parents' role in child rearing. Through this process children come to associate socially desirable behaviours with parental approval and unsocialised behaviours with parental disapproval. The association is made through the process of conditioning, as originally investigated by Pavlov. An important part of the process is that children come to associate wrong-doing with anxiety. The anticipation of anxiety acts as a kind of internal check on unsocialised behaviour, in much the same way as a burnt child dreads the fire and keeps away from it once he has learned through experience that fire is painful.

In addition to the establishing of an association between

40

unsocialised behaviours and anxiety, parents also typically reward desirable and socialised behaviours. They appear to employ the same procedures as dog handlers use to train dogs, namely rewarding behaviour which they wish to encourage. In fact the effective training of dogs and young children appears to follow the same principles. By the sensible application of these principles most parents succeed in developing in their children the disposition to behave in socialised ways.

The great majority of parents endeavour to socialise their children and use these conditioning processes to a great or lesser extent and with greater and lesser degrees of effectiveness. Inevitably some parents feel much more strongly about these matters than others and express their approval and disapproval more effectively.

A minority, such as criminal parents, may make virtually no effort to socialise their children not to steal. As a result, the children fail to acquire the usual code of respect for the property of others. In this way moral standards, or the lack of them, are transmitted through the family from one generation to the next.

6   The theory of modelling

The second mechanism through which children come to acquire their moral sense is modelling. Freud called this process identification and he meant by it that young children normally identify with or model themselves upon their parents. The leading contemporary exponent of this theory is Albert Bandura and the process is now known as modelling.[3]

Typically young children model themselves principally on the same sexed parents as themselves. This is a matter of common observation, as when little boys like to do the same things as their fathers such as servicing the car, household repairs and so forth, and little girls like to help their mothers in domestic work. These sex differences in modelling are reflected in children's play and preferences for toys, boys typically playing games involving competition and aggression and girls playing domestic and child-rearing games with dolls.

Children's tendency to model themselves on the same sexed parent as themselves is not confined to these sex defined roles.

Children also adapt the moral, religious and political values of their parents through modelling. Typically parents share these values, but where this is not the case children tend to model themselves more closely on the values of the same sexed parent as themselves. Modelling is therefore a second important process, additional to conditioning, through which socialised behaviour is transmitted in the family from one generation to the next.

Considered in evolutionary terms, both conditioning and modelling as mechanisms of learning have evolved because they have had survival value. Young animals need to learn what behaviour is dangerous, such as wandering in the forest alone and eating poisonous foods, and what is advantageous, such as finding a resting place high up in a tree. As a mechanism for accomplishing this learning, conditioning evolved much earlier than modelling. Fish, birds and simple mammals like the rat learn quite readily by conditioning but they are not capable of modelling. Learning by modelling appears only to have evolved in the monkeys and apes during the course of the last 20 million years or so and is therefore of quite recent evolutionary origin. Learning by modelling is in many ways more efficient than learning by conditioning. The young animal simply observes how its parents and other adults behave and copies them. It does not have to undergo the dangers which are frequently involved in conditioning. For instance, if the only mechanism of learning was conditioning, the young monkey would actually have been mauled by a tiger before he acquired a fear of tigers. With the development of modelling the young monkey observes that older monkeys in the troop climb up trees very quickly when they sight a tiger. The young monkey models this behaviour and does the same. Hence, learning by modelling has been a relatively recent evolutionary development which has supplemented learning by conditioning.

7   Socialisation by schools

In addition to parents, schools are also agents of socialisation, particularly in regard to socialisation for work effort and achievement. The effectiveness of schools in this respect has almost certainly diminished during the last few decades. In the first half of the century, schools administered rewards for good academic work in the form of marks and prizes, placement in the A stream and so forth, while at the same time the award of poor marks and placement in the C stream served as symbolic punishments for the lack of academic achievement.

Schools also provided role models of successful former pupils for the present generation of pupils to emulate. At Eton there are busts of old Etonian prime ministers and lists of the most academically outstanding twenty boys of each year. In my own grammar school there were rolls of honour in the form of impressive looking lists, inscribed on boards and hung in the corridors, setting out the names of former pupils who had won scholarships to Oxford and Cambridge. There must have been many small boys who looked at these lists, as I did, and determined that one day their own names would be added to them. They served as models.

These socialisation pressures for achievement have been greatly relaxed in the post World War Two decades, at any rate in the maintained schools. The award of marks and prizes, the publication of lists of examination successes and failures, streaming by ability into A, B and C classes, all these have now largely disappeared in the state comprehensives. Socialisation for academic achievement has become blunted. This is undoubtedly one reason why there is so much public dissatisfaction with academic standards in the maintained schools and why parents have been increasingly switching their children into the private sector. The maintained schools will have to do more to strengthen their socialisation functions if they are to regain public confidence.

8   The influence of heredity

Parents are not always successful in their efforts to rear well-socialised children. Although parents may attempt conscientiously to train their children and through their behaviour provide suitable models, nevertheless their children sometimes develop into drop outs, drug addicts or criminals or behave in other disappointing and unsatisfactory ways. That these misfortunes can occur has been recognised for many centuries as a hazard of parenthood. Even the best socialised and conscientious of parents produce, from time to time, the black sheep.

In recent years it has become clearly established that the black sheep phenomenon results largely from genetic factors. Since socialisation is acquired by learning processes, children can be born with a poor capacity for this kind of learning, just as they can be born with a poor capacity for school learning or for sports, or with poor health. The importance of hereditary predisposition is clearly evident from the range of socialisation outcomes commonly observable among children brought up in the same family. These are exposed to broadly the same socialisation pressures and models, yet quite frequently they develop into different personalities and this is principally due to their having been born with their own unique temperaments and learning potentialities.

One of the most useful sources of evidence on the significance of hereditary factors comes from studies of adopted children. The most thorough investigations have been carried out in Denmark by S.A. Mednick and his associates.[4] They studied some 14,000 adopted children and obtained the criminal records of their natural parents, their adopted parents and of the children themselves. The results showed that the adopted children were more likely to become criminals when their natural parents had been criminals, and they resembled their natural parents more closely than their adoptive parents in this regard. This effect can only have been due to hereditary transmission of criminal propensities. The influence of hereditary disposition on socialisation appears to be substantial.

9   Conclusions

The traditional view of the nature of children is expressed in the Christian doctrine of original sin. This states that children are naturally prone to selfish and anti-social behaviour. It is the task of parents and society to tame these propensities.

In psychology this is known as the problem of socialisation. Leading contemporary theorists in psychology adhere to the traditional original sin view. It is held that the socialisation of children is achieved principally by parents. The mechanisms are those of conditioning and modelling. Socialisation is also carried out in schools, but these are much less effective than in former decades in

44

socialising children for work effort. Hereditary factors play some role in the socialisation process and parents should not necessarily blame themselves when their efforts to socialise their children fail to achieve satisfactory results.

Notes and References

1. L. Kohlberg and E. Turiel (eds.), *Recent Research in Moral Development*, Holt, Rinehart and Loinston, 1973.
2. H.J. Eysenck, *Crime and Personality*, Routledge & Kegan Paul, 1977.
3. A. Bandura, *Social Learning Theory*, Prentice Hall, 1978.
4. S.A. Mednick, W.F. Gabrielli and B. Hutchings, 'Genetic influences in criminal convictions', *Science*, 1984, no. 224, pp. 891–894.

4   From Mephistopheles to the Corner Shop: The Decline of Moral Guidance

Errol Mathura

1   Summary and Introduction

The spirit I, that endlessly denies.
And rightly too; for all that comes to birth
is fit for overthrow, as nothing worth;
Wherefore the world were better sterilized;
Thus all that's here is evil recognised
Is gain to me, and downfall, ruin, sin
The very element I prosper in.[1]

We live in a period when 'change', not improvement, is the governing ideology. This means that experience, traditions and even reflections about the past, are discounted and ridiculed. The future, which possesses the powerful merit of immunity to examination, with all its cheating hopes, is the rage. The Golden Age is no longer in the past, but in the future. Given these assumptions, it is easy to argue, as many do, that moral education should be separated from religious education, on the ground that those children who reject Christian theology, will also reject Christian morality, and so be left without any moral foundation whatever. The new morality advocated is one in which impersonal standards are disregarded in preference for personal predelictions and morality becomes a mere matter of conscience. The slogan is that 'Circumstances alter cases' and situational variables are to be weighed against other situational variables. There is to be no frame of reference outside or above oneself. All is relative. Moral relativism is now the blessed route to personal development and moral autonomy; a route assisted by the semi-profession of the uncommitted: Counsellors.

2   Inner compulsion for change

In order to understand why, in many areas of schooling, everything that comes to birth is for overthrow, it is necessary to examine this malign obsession of our age – the need for change, the need for radical re-appraisal, the need for innovation, the inner compulsion 'to change attitudes' and the programmed disposition to be provocative. We are constantly bullied in sibilant tones by the 'Catalogue Aria' that 'we live in a period of unprecedented social change'. Yet, it has been the conceit of every age to believe that it is the more crisis prone than other times; a splendid example of reason guided by imagination, which in turn is prompted by vanity.

The zeal for this view has added nothing to the evidence. It is a notion which both satisfies and misleads. There have indeed been vast and innovative technological changes and development, but they have been largely incremental: larger units, greater speed, more intricate or simple, greater investments and more efficiency, perhaps. But no change in this century has been as radical as the foundation of the railways and the development of the factory. Indeed, large areas of 'rapid social change' have appeared incrementally in these two fields: transportation and work. Education by the state is a direct consequence of the latter. In communications, direct dialling is a linear descendant of the Morse Code.

3   Moral ideas do not have to change because technology changes

In any case, moral ideas or changes in moral ideas, which underpin and energise our behaviour, cannot be derived from technological changes, 'rapid' or not. Values cannot be derived from facts. To argue, as many do, that these 'rapid technological changes' are the causes of our current moral malaise, is to argue perversely; it is to argue from effect to cause. To cross the Atlantic by either sail or Concorde in no way diminishes the need for us to keep our promises, speak the truth, substitute argument for violence or respect the property of others. If anything, it serves to reinforce those very qualities.

In the past, as we learned to walk and talk, so we were taught rules of conduct, by some figure of authority – parent or guardian.

There were no analyses into our cognitive development, but rather an emphasis on our behaviour. Moral goodness was understood to be the child of habit. It was the sustained, habitual and continuous doing of right actions which creates and builds up a disposition to act correctly; so that the set of habits derived from childhood served, with modifications, for the rest of our lives. Many of these rules consisted in some affective concern for others, in imagining oneself to be in the shoes of another, in facing and accepting the consequences of our own actions. Rights were counterposed with responsibilities and duties: speaking the truth or working hard at school, were their own rewards. Rules, and therefore constraints, were internalised, and it is only by acting against constraints that abilities develop or genius flowers. Without rules – constraints – or conventions, in art or life, there can be no communications; similarly, without rules in a game, spectators and players alike would find the activity meaningless.

However, in the post-war years, academe has intruded into moral education in schools; and the academic philosopher's fear of authoritarianism has put authority in schools under grave suspicion – this is not the first time that fear has generated policy – in spite of the fact that reference to authority is a necessary condition for the growth of our experience. 'What shall I read?', 'Whom shall I consult?', 'Have I got it right?', 'What ought I to do now?', are all questions a learner sensibly asks of an authority when he is in doubt. Hence reference to authority is more likely to enhance than diminish or impoverish experience. Authority is a function of persons, of individuals, not institutions and it is no doubt for this reason that it is opposed by the collectivists in our midst. The exercise of the personal aspects of authority, particularly in the transmission of moral rules is a breach of the over-socialised view of man.

4   The change from 'national man' to 'social man'

One of the more emphatic shifts accompanying the growth and colonialism of sociology – allegedly the key to modern criticism and understanding – has been the replacement of the concept of 'rational man' with that of 'social man'. This shift in concept has meant that reasons for action are now creatively obscured. Young Poohwinnie is a truant. We cannot understand why before we interview young Poohwinnie's parents, which cannot be done before we talk to young Poohwinnie's peer-group, which will be inconclusive before we have the social services' report, which cannot be understood before...more research has been undertaken... We are gradually getting to the point when we will have too much information to act! This conceptual shift has permitted us to cut the knot between action and its consequences, and thus prevents individuals from growing up. Individual responsibility is now communal responsibility, and if the community is responsible, then no one is responsible, and if no one is responsible, there can be no punishment. Once the related concepts of punishment and responsibility are banished, there is a vacuum which social scientists, always vigilant for the firm perfection of an unthumbed fruit, have filled with the thesis that all our current difficulties are due to the fact that 'we are living in a period of unprecedented social and technological change'. Of course, for the social scientist, change is equated with improvement; the product of a minor understanding.

5   The drift in religious education

In religious education, there has been a perceptible slide in nomenclature from: Scripture to Religious Instruction, then a quiet descent to Religious Knowledge, which yielded to Religious Education and has now levelled out into the communal rivers of change and inevitably run into the sands as Personal and Social or Moral Studies. All these changes have been designed to avoid any hint that religious education is in any way connected with the possibility of pursuing a religious commitment. Popularisers soon move from interpretation to deception.

One advocate,[2] unable to discard the cloying principle of compulsory 'newness', a progeny of an old tradition, assures us that:

Disillusionment with society and a demand for "personal freedom" seem to have a cause and effect relationship. Current forms of expression of this feeling include "dropping out", rebelling against (especially through sex, drugs, pornography and violence) and experimenting with alternative forms of living, such as that of the Commune. The pervasive philosophy of "do your own thing", especially evident in pop-culture, represents a serious attempt to restate in contemporary terms, the value of personal identity and personal choice and so correct the imbalance created by the technological emphasis of society.[3]

6 Reflections on the concept of 'dropping-out'

What conceivably could 'dropping-out' mean in practical terms? What does the young skinhead, who is allegedly, like Plato, 'disillusioned with society' do precisely? He cannot 'drop-out' of society, as Aristotle's view on the impossibility of such a choice has remained uncontested for over two thousand years. Indeed, if he were to do so, in what context would he be 'restating in contemporary terms, the values of personal indentity and personal choice' so distorted by the technological emphasis of society? In fact, he will be on the dole, financed by taxes taken by coercion from the rich and poor alike. He will use society's sewer system, water supply, electricity distribution; its roads, parks, gardens, its buses, trains, its hospitals, shops and vast tracts of its culture; weights and measures for his drug supplies (which acutely depend on technological developments in chemistry), coinage; not to mention pornography (a product of the state of the art in marketing and photography and distribution) and, of course, a permissive value system which provides him with a clutch of semi-professionals – social workers, counsellors, out-reach workers, enablers, facilitators, resources persons and various co-ordinating personnel – all morally neutral and non-judgmental, who have formed a coalition to ensure his continued immaturity which has become the very basis of their professional and career development. In fact, our skinhead, with his culture of 'do your own thing', a severe kind of moral vandalism, has clearly signalled to the society with which he is 'disillusioned' that he is prepared to consume but not to contribute; that he is, and intends to be, a parasite. And Mr. Grimmitt bringing great intellectual resources to bear, in his hunt for novelty, on an issue which is simplicity itself, has assured us that parasitism, the blatant execution of a predatory urge, upon the rich and poor, the sick and heal-

50

thy alike – surely a democratic onslaught – represents a serious attempt to restate in contemporary terms, the values of personal identity and personal choice.

It is one of the silent rewards of literacy to discover how quickly the trendy acquire a vocabulary in excess of their needs and are consequently never at a loss for the wrong word. Mr. Grimmitt has resorted to the Liberal cant phrase, 'personal freedom', with a sense of repose, making it the subject of a demand, rather than the object of a quest. Even more questionable is the notion of 'dropping-out' which, in practise, means dropping-in on the Welfare State, while simultaneously asserting a refusal to make any contribution.

'Experimenting' with alternative forms of living certainly suggests a scientific approach: the possession of a hypothesis to disprove, an agreed methodology or public criteria for failure, but which in fact – and Mr Grimmitt must know this – is merely indicative of a parasitism at a more intense and soporific level. How could anyone stupified with drugs, alcohol, sex and violence, conceivably be described as 'experimenting'? 'Disillusioned with society' is a hypothesis dear to all good liberals and held in caressing indulgence, which it is impossible to discard, since it covers so many imaginary calamities. This sustained descent into parasitic hedonism, accompanied by the quiet destruction of all moral values, represents for Mr Grimmitt, the search for personal growth. Unlike Shakespeare, he seems to have lacked the challenge of a vulgar audience.

7 Faith and the Corner Shop mentality in religious education

Some further observations convinced Mr Grimmitt of 'even further need for a radical re-appraisal of our thinking about religious teaching.' On the question of 'faith' with an undirected and unassisted understanding he assures us that:

> If the word "faith" is equated with religious belief, even in a broad sense, then we are restricting the child to one distinctive world view.[4]

The argument is transient and confuses teaching one view with restricting the child to one view. In any case this Head of RE in a teacher-training college, seems himself bereft of faith. He writes:

> It is just as questionable to infer that there is merit in having a "faith" – any faith – as it is to infer the merits of a particular faith.[5]

Like the pre-Socratic Greeks, our author would rather assert a doubt than frame a proposition; function is killed by surmise. He continues:

> If RE Teachers could adopt the attitude of a shopkeeper with wares in his window which he is anxious for customers to examine, appreciate and even "try-on" but not feel any obligation to buy, then many of the educational problems connected with RE would disappear.[6]

This secular journey from theology to the corner shop was almost predictable. The resort to metaphors such as 'try-on' and 'buy', is carefully mistaken for analysis and, worse, for description. Just imagine 'trying-on' Judaism: would one start with Deuteronomy or Leviticus? Or should one 'appreciate' the Sharia Law of Islam, which provides for the stoning to death of adulterers, but 'with no obligation to buy'. These views are untouched by even the most latent scepticism. In a dash for modernity, we are told that 'Nothing could be less attuned to the demands of contemporary theology' than the acceptance and use by children, of traditional Christian formularies. Our author resents any attempts at the inculcation of favourable attitudes to religion:

> It is not possible to avoid "loading" this approach with a particular set of beliefs and values and simply to concentrate on providing the child with an opportunity to explore a whole number of alternative "frames of reference" atheistic as well as theistic.[7]

According to this doctrine, which implies that all entrance tickets to past beliefs and values have been sold, and which insists on the pressing need to make everything 'relevant and meaningful to the 20th century', children must be taught to doubt before they can have faith, the possession of which is questionable, anyway. But surely, the store-keeper, with his wares in the window, is most likely to have a 'loss-leader', perhaps cheaper five pound bags of sugar, a 'best choice for today' or an 'unbeatable bargain', in fact, a 'loaded' approach. If the store-keeper, Mr Grimmitt's ideal example, is permitted to have a 'loaded' approach, then why deny it to the religious teacher. The advocacy of a neutral approach is equally value-laden and thus also 'loaded'.

So the child will be permitted to 'explore a whole number of alternative frames of reference' without any preparation – no reading, no instruction, no values, prejudices or firmly held beliefs. His approach is to be based on pooled ignorance; his relationship to these 'alternative frames of reference' must be that of a coin to a slot-machine. Such is the phoney democratic vigilance against convictions. The past, and Mr. Grimmit's past too, presumably, must be repudiated. Like Julius Caesar, one must kick the ladder by which one ascended. Progress is linear and unfettered and, like shopping, can be planned, implemented and has all the charms of demonstrability. There is no social bank of 'right' and 'wrong' in which communal surpluses of values are kept for dissemination among the young. They must, of their own accord, discover virtue and vices and perhaps stumble upon the principle and efficacy of queueing. Each new generation will consist of moral vagrants, who will project upon their surroundings the menace of their own indiscipline as they move forward in their 'serious attempt to restate in contemporary terms the value of personal identity'.

In the world of those who suffer from such internal disequilibrium, which could only be righted from the bottle of radicalism, to put questions before understanding, the young must, like the editor of *Playboy*, create a world in their own image. In fact it is the genesis of self-centredness:

> Since self-centredness is the essence of life, the overcoming of self-centredness is the most difficult spiritual task that any living creature can set himself. Conscience commands a human being to understand this task, and it gives the command with authority which is absolute. Conscience imposes the job, but it does not provide the tools.[8]

8   The role of the past in overcoming self-centredness

To provide the tools for overcoming self-centredness is the purpose of the past, that vast repository of all our accumulated doings, both evident and mysterious, hidden and explicit, in the crevices of our daily lives: in philosophy, religion and the schools. The certain prescription for overcoming self centredness is death, but rather than a final solution, one must seek some provisional methods, like the management of desires, the elimination of which is the basis of Buddhism, Stoicism and Epicureanism. In the 'do your own thing', non-judgmental atmosphere, where the development of ideas is always from the individual to society, never the reverse, the self-transcending desires of love, compassion and sympathy are unlikely to prosper. Freedom is never ascetic. Schools bring conspicuously little zeal to the issues of values or moral behaviour. What is more, the central preoccupation with the social gospel means dispensing with the importance of individual responsibility. One cannot both fulminate against classes and attitudes and address men and women to their particular duties. The urge to assert a right has become meaningless by its monotony which is matched by a common reticence on individual responsibility. The idea that no one could have a 'right' without someone accepting an obligation has come to appear quite perverse.

9   The search for autonomy

The prevailing mood is for autonomy, the autonomous pupil, a substantially mistaken concept which has graduated into a myth and has since degenerated into a strategy; and the error is concealed in the language of inspiration. Whether human beings are indeed autonomous from birth or whether their potentiality unfolds spontaneously later, it would render any education to promote autonomy superfluous and the only method recognised would be that of self-discovery. But this would make it impossible for the cumulative achievement of knowledge and skill to be passed from one generation to the next. It would also be impossible to apply any public criteria to the quality of what the individual discovered for himself. And in the absence of such criteria, it would be impossible to say whether what the individual had discovered for himself was either false, biased or insignificant. Autonomy is not an achievement; it is a matter of degree; it indicates an attitude of mind rather than an achieved state. In the moral sphere, the lives of reasonable autonomous people are governed by a large basket of rules on which there has been very little reflection, and which have been inherited like a family heirloom. Indeed, those who have attained a fair degree of moral autonomy in their moral lives, are seldom moral innovators – a fundamental error in liberal thought resulting from the inner drive to confuse participation with creation.

10   Counselling: a quite misguided enterprise

This drive for autonomy has fostered the semi-profession of counselling. The counsellor is now an ubiquitous figure in the realm of education but he must never give advice:

> You will probably be asked for advice – "What do you think I should do?" You may feel a lot of pressure to supply it and will be tempted because it is an obvious way of appearing to be helpful.

But don't give it; it is certain to breach their maturity, and in any case:

> Advice is quite likely to be unsatisfactory no matter how good it sounds to you, and while it may bring some short term benefits, it does little to strengthen people's power over their lives. So help instead by encouraging them to be specific about their experiences, feelings, attitudes, and look realistically at the options open to them.

So, if advice may bring some 'short-term benefits' we must deny it to the supplicant, as it might ('might' implies might not) impair the serious development of autonomy. We must 'look realistically at the options' but be very careful as 'it is easy to dress up advice as information' – Though it is arguably harder to get a job if you haven't got A Levels and there are indeed arguments for staying on at College one should beware of suggesting this. One must contain oneself. Nothing, not even the truth, must be allowed to impede the development of autonomy.

The Counsellor cannot attempt to balance his duty to his client with some conception of his duty to his institution or to his society. The client's interests are paramount and employing Institutions need to understand this. For example, it is not part of a counsellor's role to influence a client against sexually promiscuous behaviour or against solving his problems by theft.[10]

Notice the moral authoritarianism of the author, the Stalinist disposition, determined to create duties and responsibilities for others, to mark boundaries for society, institutions and employers 'who have a need to understand' their right to do such things, while portentuously insisting on the 'ethical neutrality about the process of counselling.' One's bank of experience is forbidden to the client, our moral dispositions must be concealed, our emotions frozen, any sense of outrage hidden. Our silence on the client's sexually promiscuous behaviour or his disposition to thieving, is hardly likely to discourage him from such behaviour; but then it is precisely this behaviour pattern which provides the need for more counsellors. Even Socrates sought advice and guidance without the slightest breach of his autonomy:

> Cephalus: ...so don't refuse me, but come and talk to the young men here and visit us as if we were old friends.
> Socrates: As a matter of fact, Cephalus, I enjoy talking to very old men, for they have gone before us, as it were, on a road that we too most probably tread, and it seems to me that we can find out from them what it is like and whether it is rough and difficult or broad and easy. You are now at an age when you are, as the poets say, about to cross the bar, and I would like to find out from you what you have to tell us. Is it a difficult time of life or not?[11]

Counsellors seem to have great difficulties with the management of truth. They are forbidden to tell a client that his chances of employment might be better if he had A Levels, not because it is untrue, but because it suggests that he should stay at college. They are instructed not to disapprove of their client's thieving or promiscuity, coupled with the further injunction:

> ...he must recognise too that his client may lack the strength of mind to face certain highly unpalatable truths about himself and

must refrain therefore, from bringing certain self-awareness until he has helped him to find the strength to bear them.[12]

How precisely is one to know when someone has the strength to bear an unpalatable truth about themselves unless it it told to them? 'Like the doctor, the Counsellor, accepts at all times the first law of his profession: Thou shalt do no harm.'[13] That is, the Counsellor must no cause suffering. This desire arises from the gently nurtured growth of a standardised sensibility. Counselling has developed from a sensitivity which is unhappy with the world, not because it is monotonous, ugly, lacking in virtue or heroism, or because all things are emphemeral, but because it contains suffering; and institutions are to be the agents of individual happiness. Counsellors understand; morality condemns and autonomy secures authenticity. Happiness has become doctrinaire.

However, the maintenance of ethical neutrality, and the retention of a non-judgmental attitude to clients, admits of onc exception – racism.

Every school should have a clearly and publicly stated policy against all forms of racism and a defined procedure for dealing with it. Counselling may also be required for the individuals involved for victims as well as instigators, though this should on no account take the place of disciplinary action.[14]

This intentional double-standard is the crowning bloom in the hot house of Liberalism. Gone are all those rosy qualities with which Counsellors were endowed:

Tolerance for human fallibility; one should want to understand people and be optimistic at all times about their capacity for growth. One is not interested in condemning them. One has faith in the perfectibility of man.

11 Cultural distinctions accepted in other fields so why not in religion and morals?

The role of moral education in schools has been subverted by the search for autonomy. Choice – 'what ought I to do?' – has become the subject of individual fiat. But we are not private individuals, constructing our own concepts out of the data of our raw experience. Concepts are acquired and we learn to apply them in interpreting and understanding our experience. That the 'what ought I to do?' question, is the sole business of the individual, ignores the fact that each human being develops within the context of a pre-existing world of shared meanings. The mind is not simply a given, there to be flexed like a muscle, but an achievement that largely depends on one gaining access to the inheritance of shared meanings. It is this inheritance from the past which prevents the 'radical' from creating the world in his own image and forms the basis for his rejection of the past. The 'radical' can have no conversation with the past, because his language is Esperanto, not a growth, but a construction.

The idea that young people should be inducted into a culture, be it religious or literary, with the hope that some of them may, in time, come to modify our understanding in these areas, by introducing a different and sustainable interpretation, is the basis of all genuine progress. Take cricket for instance. It has its own culture, its language and history. When youngsters or foreigners are inducted into the game, they must learn the language: 'mid-off', 'cover-point' and 'backward-square'. They will learn that the authority to change the field is transferred from the captain to the bowler. Acquaintance with the great names, famous grounds, highest scores will grow, together with the utility of the rules relating both to dress and performance. The idea that the decision of the umpire cannot be a subject for negotiation, might introduce the shock of hope that there are stable points in this changing world. Over time, great players have introduced new elements, O'Reilly the googly and Ranjitsinghi the leg-glance, for example, which have become part of the common culture of the game, into which others, in their turn, will be inducted.

Since this is so for cricket, and those accepting the LBW rule will never think of themselves as reactionary, then why not a similar induction into religion, art and literature and morals among others? How are games to be played if the rules are to be autonomously determined by individual fiat? Faced with a bowler's appeal, the umpire's question, 'What ought I to do?' merely requires a knowledge of the rules and their application to current circumstances – not 'to the contemporary needs of the 20th Century'.

When we are assured by Mr. Grimmitt that such religious concepts as 'awe', 'mystery' and 'worship' are more likely to be grasped by the young through their involvement in meeting a pop star 'than if he is presented with the story of Moses and the burning bush or told about the transfiguration' we might safely conclude that he has an axe to blunt. How does one get from Mr. Grimmitt's 'shopkeeper' to Psalm 23?

Notes and References

1. J.W. Goethe, *Faust*, Part 1, Penguin, 1949, p. 75.
2. M.A. Grimmitt, *Guide to New Approaches: What can we do in RE?*, Mayhew and McCrimmon, 1973. The author is Director of RE Resources and the In-service Training Centre at West Hill College of Education, Birmingham, pp. 12–13.
3. Ibid., pp. 12–13.
4. Ibid.
5. Ibid., p. 26.
6. Ibid.
7. Ibid., p. 25.
8. Arnold Toynbee, *Experience*, Oxford University Press, 1969, p. 150.
9. Tom Wylie, *Counselling Young People*, NYP, 1980.
10. Youth Council Advisory Service, Vol. 14, No. 1, March 1974.
11. Plato, *The Republic*, Penguin, p. 52.
12. Youth Council Advisory Service, op. cit., p. 4.
13. Ibid.
14. School Curriculum Development Committee, *Agenda for Multicultural Teaching*, Longman, 1986.
15. K.A. Strike and K. Egan, *Ethics and Educational Policy*, Routledge and Kegan Paul, 1978.

5   Young People Betrayed

David Marsland

1   Summary and Introduction

Children are not transformed into adults at the age of 18 simply because the law classifies them so. While they may be legally free of parental authority, the evidence strongly suggests that they continue to *need* adult guidance and role models for several more years. Youth is a specific phase of development, however popular it may have become for experts to deny this, and young people do have special needs which need to be recognised and catered for if they are to develop into responsible adults. But parents have been encouraged to abdicate their responsibility towards their children not only at 18 but at an ever earlier age, creating a vacuum which schools and more specialist organisations such as the Youth Service and student unions have signally failed to fill. It is crucial for a successful transition to adulthood that young people should be inculcated with sound moral principles and this can best be achieved if parental authority over older, as well as younger, children is restored.

2   Young people *need* adult authority and guidance

I recall giving a talk about the life of young people some ten years ago to a group of German conservatives. I found them as irritably resistant to my account of young people's inadequacies and lack of purpose as any average collection of *Guardian* readers, social workers, or leaders of teachers' trade unions. It is enormously difficult to tell the truth about young people and get it heard. For adults of all persuasions share a powerful vested interest in deceiving themselves about their own persistent failure in recent decades in influencing young people wisely and well. The truth must nevertheless be told, however dispiriting.

There are of course many thousands of young people leading happy and admirable lives. There are some respects in which almost all young people have progressed beyond the standards which could be expected in earlier generations. No less certainly, however, there are huge numbers of young people we have failed to save from appalling behaviour, and almost all young people in Britain have been allowed and encouraged by adults to live in some aspects of their lives by standards which are unacceptably low. For example, according to the Office of Population Censuses and Surveys, the illegitimacy rate has more than doubled in the past ten years, and now represents *above a fifth of all live births*.[1] Again, according to Home Office statistics, nearly *one in three* men born in 1953 had one or more convictions for serious crime by the age of twenty-eight.[2] And in a recent comparison of 15 year olds' arithmetic capacities, West German children did *twice as well* as British children – perhaps the German conservatives of my first paragraph had a point after all![3]

Morality, crime, and educational competence aside, sit on the top deck of any bus, north or south, inner city or suburbs, and listen to the foul language of 12 year old girls, let alone boys. The fact is that so-called progressive ideas have done at least as much damage to young people – our older children – as to pre-adolescents. The 1960s celebration of youth has provided an apparently irresistible excuse for neglecting young people's need for adult authority and guidance. They have been increasingly abandoned to the irresponsible, negative influences of the peer group, pop culture, the media, and inadequately trained teachers and youth workers.

If we are to help them instead of harming them still further, we shall need to acknowledge their immaturity, strengthen the role of parents and the family, and ensure that professionals working with them are carefully selected and properly trained. Young people need both freedom and control. Well-balanced order is essential if they are to develop into effective, happy, and mature adults.

3 Reducing the age of majority can't turn adolescents into adults overnight

It is no accident that it was at the height of the feverish era of the 'swinging sixties' that the age of majority was reduced from 21 to 18. The Latey Report – of which I have said elsewhere that it was notable for its rare combination of poverty of evidence and shallowness of argumentation – was published in 1967.[4] With almost no public discussion and scarcely any critical argument in Parliament, a Bill was enacted as if by universal consensus in 1969. Quite suddenly millions of youngsters were transformed by Parliamentary fiat into adults.

Perhaps adult anxieties about their responsibilities for young people had already by then grown to such a pitch that even without the Act older adolescents would have been abandoned in any case to their own allegedly 'independent' devices. Presumably indeed the change would not have been effected so quickly and easily unless 18 year olds were already regarded, at least by influential opinion formers, as mature adults.

But even if the lowering of the age of majority was a mere ritualistic flourish, it has proved subsequently to be a powerful symbol, signalling unambiguously to young people that parents, teachers, and other adults have washed their hands of any responsibility for their care and guidance. Moreover, with the vote, consumer rights, and moral latitude extended to 18 year olds, a campaign was immediately begun to expand a spurious independence still further to 16 year olds, 14 year olds, and even younger. In the long run the tendency is to disinvent adolescence and youth altogether, and to transform all our older children, post-puberty, into pseudo-adults.

4 Concept of adolescence sabotaged by sociologists

This tendency has been encouraged by social scientists intent on destroying the credibility of the concept of adolescence and the plausibility of any genuine understanding of the nature of youth. While they have admittedly not been alone in this mischievous work, Marxist and other socialist sociologists must take a large part of the responsibility for it.

In *Resistance through Rituals* – the most influential book about youth produced in Britain since the War – Stuart Hall, and his co-authors pushed their arguments so far as to claim inter alia that:–

- It is questionable whether youth can properly be thought of as a stage of life at all
- 'Youth as a concept is unthinkable'
- Even to think of youth as a social category 'does not make much empirical sense'
- Youth does not exist 'as a single homogeneous group' but is an 'artificial construction which runs in the face of the evidence of the social differences within generations'
- Youth should be treated as 'a secondary and dependent or determinate factor of social differentiation, a factor affecting the individual or group within those social relations which structure not just their youth but their whole life'
- 'These sets of relations are preeminently class relations'[5]

These curious assumptions, together with their antiquated Marxist under-pinnings, have been accepted wholesale by other influential sociologists, such as Paul Willis, and transmitted via university, polytechnic, and college courses to whole cohorts of teachers, social workers, probation officers, and youth and community workers.[6] The idea that adolescence is a convenient fiction designed to serve the selfish interests of adults, and that youth is entirely a social construction without any real basis in biology or psychology has also been taken up unquestioningly by the media, and transmitted widely, with all the authority of television 'documentary' and 'quality' journalism throughout the kingdom.

Yet this whole analysis is contradicted by all the reputable empirical research there is.[7] Of course the nature and meaning of adolescence and youth vary between one culture and another, between one period of history and another, and between different social groups in contemporary Britain. Of course the character of adolescence and youth has been significantly transformed by the extension of schooling and by the growth of prosperity. *Nonetheless, it is quite beyond dispute that adolescence is a real, general, and important phenomenon.* All young people, as a result of adolescence triggered by the physical transformation of puberty, are in a period of transition *between* childhood and adulthood. They are *neither* children *nor* adults, and to treat them as if they were is to deny reality and harm them cruelly.[8]

5 Comprehensive schooling fails young people

Parents have not been immune to the mistaken and mischievous ideas about young people which I have described in the previous section. In countless families – not least the most privileged in economic terms – great damage has been done and is being done as a result. However, parents are for the most part saved from extremes of folly by their everyday closeness to their children, by the fact that they are their own children, and by the opportunities which family life provides for testing and correcting even the silliest of beliefs.

Schools have none of these advantages, and it is in the contemporary secondary schooling system that the fashionable misunderstanding of youth has done the worst damage. Whatever its other advantages and disadvantages, the well-established system of grammar, secondary modern, and technical schools at least had the merit of *belief in discipline, commitment to standards of excellence*, and *positive support for competition*. These values – shared throughout the tripartite system – rested on a sensible, commonsensical understanding of the character of young people and of their special needs. All this, besides much else, has been lost with comprehensivisation.

From the start, and increasingly as they have spread and become normalised, comprehensive schools have been arenas for the display of progressivist ideas and for the flaunting of implausible but fashionable theories. Above all they have been so insistent that their pupils should not be treated 'like children' that young people in their care – misconstrued as independent adults – have been denied the frameworks of guidance and control without which young people cannot succeed in becoming adults at all:

- They are not allowed to succeed, lest it should hurt others, nor to fail, in case it might damage themselves

- Denied the opportunity of competition, in the valuable arenas of academic work and sport, they discover for themselves destructive alternatives in terms of which to measure and rate themselves in pop and sex and style
- Deprived of intellectual and moral standards and in the absence of discipline and honest guidance, they look to the peer group and pop culture for frameworks of meaning and purpose for their lives
- They are faced by wild oscillations by teachers between progressivist treatment as young adults with nothing serious still to learn, and crude authoritarianism provoked by their incapacity to spring direct from childhood to adulthood in compliance with their teachers' foolish theories. In consequence many young people lose heart altogether, and trust neither teachers nor adults in general.

One could go on. It is a long, sad story.[9] Even in the best of comprehensive schools the most important learning needs are being consistently neglected; and in many schools, particularly in the inner cities, pupils are being corrupted wholesale by teachers' headmasters' and inspectors' complete lack of understanding of young people's imperative need for leadership, purpose, and discipline.

6   A degree of competition essential for young people

The Inner London Education Authority has recently been obliged to undertake a special study and publish a lengthy report in order to persuade itself and to assure the public that it is not opposed in principle to competitive sport in its schools. Simultaneously, educationists generally (one might almost say educationists as a class) have been managing to take time out from their supposedly onerous work to campaign against the Minister of Education's modest attempt at restoring legitimacy to academic competition by introducing systematic testing into the schools.

Quite ludicrously our most renowned educational theorists, our most distinguished professors of education, and our most senior HMIs appear to have persuaded themselves that competition is quite simply a bad thing. This extraordinary belief – which is scarcely more plausible than the superstitions of Ancient Greece which caused the exile of the philosopher Anaxagoras for his suggestion that the moon was a rock – appear to have permeated the whole education system.

Progressivist ideology frowns on any competition in case some should fail and in case those who win might foolishly imagine they were somehow better than others. In fact resistance to competition, in the academic field, in sport, and in social life generally, is far more damaging to most young people than any amount of failure. Excluded from constructive competition, they find their own destructive alternatives in hooliganism, vandalism, and the parade of style. Denied the privilege of trying and failing, and trying and failing again, and trying once more, they are incapacitated for the rough and tumble of life in a dynamic free society.

7   Young people need constructive involvement under adult leadership

As much as competition, young people need involvement. The schools have foolishly denied them competition on principle, which is bad enough, but they have explicitly *promised* them involvement, and failed to deliver it – which is even worse. Increasingly young people have been abandoned over the past 30 years to their own devices in the futile milieu of peer groups. Out of class, out of mind it seems.

Truancy is massive in scale, and in many schools entirely condoned.[10] Senior pupils are powerfully encouraged to 'do their own thing' when formal schooling can dispense with them. Before and after examinations it has become customary for pupils to 'truant' officially for long periods. The valuable British tradition of extra-curricular activities has been gravely weakened by the unwillingness of unionised teachers to work beyond normal hours. The whole nature of extra-curricular activities has been subverted by the tendency of teachers to deride 'elitist' pursuits such as music and drama and the competitive spirit of sport.

Overall, pupils' experience of schooling has been progressively attenuated, and reduced in the end to the reluctant necessities of low-level academic learning construed merely instrumentally. Yet effective development of young people *absolutely requires their active involvement under adult leadership in useful and satisfying endeavour.* This should of course include academic learning, but for most if not all young people it needs to extend much beyond this.

Both work experience and community involvement should be much more strongly developed, with extra-curricular activities restored and strengthened. It is in these arenas that teachers can most successfully harness young people's natural urge to be active and useful. It is through involvement in practical and genuinely useful action in the community and in the work place that young people can most effectively learn all the lessons from which they are currently being deliberately shielded: discipline, self-discipline, courtesy, co-operation, effort, enterprise, competition, and independence.

8   Training schemes not the dole for unemployed young people

Large-scale youth unemployment is a major negative influence in young people's lives. Abandoning them in their thousands to enforced leisure on the streets, and paying them for the dubious privilege of it is a nonsense and a scandal.

In my view the Youth Training Scheme is a promising constructive alternative. However, it has been consistently resisted and sabotaged by the left and by the youth lobby, and it needs to be substantially improved and strengthened. Certainly benefits should be refused to 16 to 18 year olds who refuse to take advantage of available training schemes. There are, moreover, other changes that are needed, not least gradual extension beyond 18 to take in the whole category of youth unemployment from 16 to 24. Employers should be expected to pay more attention than they for the most part have done to the special needs of their young employees, and to participate more actively in YTS.

I have argued elsewhere that the tragedy of youth unemployment is an opportunity which the Government should seize to transform radically the whole social situation of youth.[11] We need a flexible package – available to all young people – of academic education, vocational training, general education, work experience, and community service. Within this framework, financial support would be available to young people – but only in return for active involvement in relevant components of the whole programme. Idle unemployment would be outlawed. *All* young people would have a real opportunity and a serious obligation to improve themselves, strengthen their social competence, and advance themselves as far as each was capable.

If a programme of this sort were organised within a national framework in all the localities, linking school, college, work, and community together, the complaints of some young people about 'government schemes', which are seen by many as second best alternatives to real work, would be rapidly dissipated. We should have a system of positive youth development appropriate to a free society to replace the existing chaotic charter for neglect and licence. I take up the principles which should inform this programme, and the special role of the concept of social education within it in my conclusion.

9   The Youth Service politicised, to the neglect of its proper role

The Youth Service is funded from the public purse to address and answer precisely the problems of and with young people which I have described earlier. A locally organised component of (in most cases) the education service, it provides and supports youth clubs, youth centres, youth projects, and youth counselling facilities. It is staffed by a cadre of professionally-trained youth and community workers and a much larger body of voluntary and part-time paid assistants. Its purpose is to complement the work of the formal educational system by the provision of social education for young people aged 14 to 21.

Despite considerable achievements – particularly through the great voluntary movements which it incorporates and co-ordinates, and in work with the most disadvantaged young people in the inner cities – the Youth Service has not, in my judgement, lived up to its promise, or successfully tackled the challenges it has taken on. A whole series of official reports – Albemarle in 1960, Milson-Fairbairn in 1969, and Thompson as recently as 1982[12] – have served merely to confirm the extent of confusion about basic purposes and lack of positive vision among the leadership of the Youth Service.

Youth work training has been largely subverted by the mistaken theories of youth I have criticised earlier. Curricula tend increasingly to be shaped not by a realistic understanding of the special problems of adolescence or sensible, practical principles designed to enable youth workers to offer young people genuine help, but by the irrelevant and sectarian assumptions of feminism, black pseudo-radicalism, reverse sexism, and extremist leftism. Youth workers have tended to align themselves unthinkingly with supposedly progressive ideas, and allowed themselves to become identified as part of the 'radical' left, rather than as a useful professional group including people with diverse political views. Youth officers, whose responsibility is planning and management of the Service, have with rare exceptions provided weak and vacillating leadership, and allowed youth work to drift towards a merely political role of advocacy for the interests of young people, with these interests themselves defined in a narrow and sectarian way. Instead of providing solutions for the youth problems, the Youth Service has sadly become a part of the problem itself, and a largely negative factor in the contemporary crisis of youth.[13]

10   Student unions have done little to prepare members for life in the real world

When the authors of the Albemarle Report were successfully urging the expansion of provision for ordinary young people through the Youth Service, a key element in their arguments was comparison with the situation of student youth and the generous facilities afforded to them through student unions. Their arguments in this respect were largely valid. Sadly, however, the considerable public resources expended on student unions have been largely wasted, and to a significant extent counter-productive.

Much of this resource has been squandered, as a result of the activities of the National Union of Students, on irrelevant left-wing political campaigning. Much more has been wasted, just as extravagantly if less destructively, on facilities for entertainment and recreation which commercial organisations could provide more efficiently and less expensively without any call on public funds.

While focussing on these negative distractions of left-wing politics and mere fun, the Unions have done next to nothing in the way of positive socially responsible leadership of young people. The huge numbers of highly privileged young people in the student body have been offered in consequence precious little help with the serious problems of preparation for life in the real world of modern society which all young people, however privileged, unavoidably face. Almost as much as the mass of ordinary young people, and the minority of the seriously disadvantaged, our student elite has been abandoned for two generations to the negative influences of the peer group, pop culture, and political subversion.

11 Young people reflect adult society – they need a good example

The organisations whose betrayal of young people I have so far criticised – the schools, the colleges, employers, the Youth Service, and the student unions – have not been operating in a cultural vacuum. Their damaging effects on young people have been allowed and encouraged by the ethos of permissivism inaugurated in the sixties and unchallenged even during the Thatcher years.

The immoralism prevalent in the mass media and the shoddy example set for young people by adult role models in all walks of life are primary causes of the desperate condition of many young people's lives. In relation to drugs, sex, crime, self-discipline, and manners, the examples offered by leading figures in politics, the professions, the churches, and the media have been and continue to be appalling. No less harmful is the cowardly unwillingness of leaders to speak out in condemnation of bad behaviour. Low morals drive out high morals as effectively as bad money drives out good money, and it is young people who are left with the debased currency of immoralism as a result – and then we blame *them* for it!

There is little scope at all for reforming the institutions responsible for young people's care and development unless and until we manage as a nation to achieve at least a degree of re-moralisation of social life. We have to challenge immoralist permissivism with beliefs and values to which young people can commit themselves positively and actively.

12   Restore responsibility for young people to their families as first step towards social education

A crusading effort at cultural re-moralisation such as this will no doubt seem to many an implausible objective in the late 1980s, and to some perhaps itself morally unacceptable. Moral arguments aside for the moment,[14] it is certainly likely to be a very difficult endeavour. All the more so if we fail to recognise that over and above a transformation of values, cultural revolution requires structural changes in institutions and social practices if it is to succeed in practice. In particular we shall need, I believe, to see:-

- Substantial withdrawal by the state from its power over young people's lives
- Reform of the system of incentives and rewards for young people's various activities
- Restoration of families' financial and moral responsibility for their own young people

I have presented these arguments fully elsewhere, and will not go into them further here.[15] I conclude by touching briefly on an idea which I believe provides the essential link between general cultural change and structural reform on the one hand and the possibility of radical improvements in the public institutions responsible for young people's development on the other. *This is social education.* The elements of my analysis and their linkages are shown in fig. 1.

From time to time the media or political leaders are provoked by some extreme of youthful folly or wickedness to demand the restoration of the sort of tight control on young people's behaviour which was still normal as recently as the 1930s. After a flurry of speeches it is usually recognised that the re-imposition of antique authoritarian controls is for all practical purposes simply impossible. It is also, in my view, undesirable. It is not proving feasible even within the authoritarian ideological frameworks of communism or Islam.[16] In an ideological context of democracy and individualism – in short in any genuinely modern society – authori-

Fig. 1: A programme for youth development

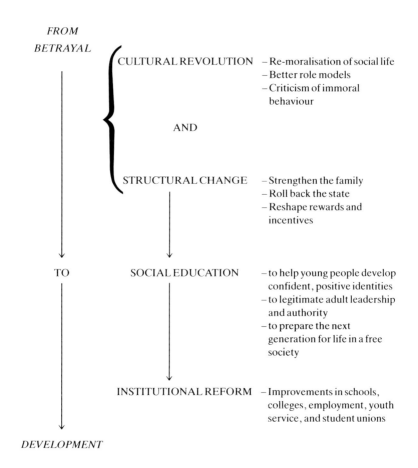

tarian control of young people is as morally unacceptable as it is practically infeasible.

13   Social education essential for successful development into adulthood

Yet on the other hand there is – and has to be if things are not to get even worse in regard to young people's relations with society – a serious alternative to the corrupting licence into which we have fallen in reaction against our earlier primitive authoritarianism. *The crux of this alternative is provided by the concept of social education.*[17]

Social education is essentially a process through which adults are enabled to offer to young people that confident, effective leadership which they both need and seek by way of support in their transition between childhood and adulthood. At local and national levels we need to see established urgently a public service committed explicitly to the social education of all young people. This service should support the family and the schools and colleges in preparing young people realistically for life in a competitive democratic society. It should equip them with the moral principles and capacities for enterprising self-reliance which life in a free society demands.

A more specific purchase on the objectives of social education can be obtained by using Leslie Button's taxonomy of young people's needs.[18] He argues – following the main line of developmental psychology – that young people have to answer certain needs adequately if they are to navigate youth – the transition between childhood and adulthood – successfully. These are:-

- The need for new experience
- The need for relationships with peers
- The need for association with the opposite sex
- The need for significance
- The need for a coherent world view
- The need to come to terms with authority

On Button's analysis, the objective of social education is to help young people answer these several needs *in order to facilitate the growth of mature autonomy.* He believes that young people cannot, for the most part, in contemporary social conditions, answer these needs adequately and win through to mature autonomy without the sort of positive adult support and honest guidance which social education properly understood can offer them. Some few may be fortunate enough to find such help accidentally and by good luck, sometimes from an individual teacher of outstanding quality, sometimes from a youth worker doing constructive social education as it were unawares, and sometimes from their parents. For the most part, however, young people need a systematic opportunity for working through these normal developmental problems such as only social education programmes can provide. Many of our young people – and not by any means only or even particularly those from backgrounds which are disadvantaged in simple economic or cultural terms – are deprived of this opportunity. It is the mission of social education to provide it on a general basis for all young people.

14   Adolescence: a distinct phase of development with distinct needs

These objectives are entirely compatible with what is in my judgement the most sophisticated and penetrating analysis of youth currently available, that offered by Erik Erikson, in *Childhood and Society* and throughout his work.[19] Erikson argues that each age and stage of life presents to everyone a developmental psychological crisis which has to be worked through effectively if positive growth is to continue. He proposes that in adolescence and youth there is a general problem to be faced about *identity*. He has described adolescence as

> a time of "identity crisis" in which the individual must shape a positive, industrious, sociable, and forward-looking self from the flux of personal change. The adolescent is faced with a plastic future in which the options seem almost unlimited and the outcome unclear.

This period of confusion arises both out of psychological development, being triggered by the onset of puberty, and as a result of socio-cultural forces.

For, in modern society at least, adolescence is marked by what Erikson calls 'a psycho-social moratorium' – a period of 'escape and release' in relation to the forces of socialisation. During this period young people have to work out for themselves their identity crisis in order to achieve mature autonomy. The task of social educators is to help them with this stressful process. Thus social education is concerned fundamentally with assisting in the development in individual young people of optimal identity, self-esteem, confidence, and social competence. It is no more – and no less – than active adult participation in helping young people to face and handle the normal developmental tasks of adolescence and youth, and to adjust positively and creatively to adulthood.

All young people in all circumstances need and deserve the help which social education offers. In this period of our history – when the whole structure of our society is being buffeted by a technological and economic transformation at least as far-reaching as the Industrial Revolution – the necessity for social education is even more compelling. If we can provide effective programmes of social education aiming coherently and unambiguously at the purposes I have suggested here, and staffed by men and women guided by sound moral principles we shall at least have the chance of offering them the help they need. Without it, there is only pain for young people and trouble for society ahead.

15   Above all young people must be given good role models

By way of conclusion, one last and crucial point. We do not know yet precisely how young people are influenced in positive directions as a result of social education. Probably clarity about objectives, effective management, and skilled use of a wide range of methods and techniques are essential. One thing at least seems certain. *The quality of social educators as persons makes all the difference.* For, even in their rebellious negativism towards adults in general, and their parents in particular, which is the hallmark of adolescence, young people are all of them continuously assessing potential role models, and seeking from among the adults society presents them with exemplars of the qualities and values they might themselves choose to emulate. If social educators are scruffy, cynical, and negative, if they are themselves confused about their values, if they demonstrate no joy in life, or positive feelings about the future and about the potential our society offers – then social education will fail, and young people will turn elsewhere for the adult help and leadership they all need and deserve.[20]

Notes and References

1. Office of Population Censuses and Surveys, 1988, reported in *Daily Telegraph*, 13 January 1988.
2. *Social Trends*, HMSO, 1986, page 189.
3. Reported in the *Mail On Sunday*, 16 August, 1987.
4. Report of the Committee on the Age of Majority, HMSO, Cmnd. 3342, 1967.
5. S. Hall and T. Jefferson (eds.), *Resistance through Rituals*, Hutchinson, 1976; quotations from S. Hall et al., 'Youth a Stage of Life?', *Youth in Society*, No. 17, 1976.
6. P. Willis, *Learning to Labour*, Saxon House, 1977, and *Profane Culture*, RKP, 1978. Also M. Brake, *The Sociology of Youth Culture and Youth Sub-cultures*, RKP, 1981. A critical account of such views is presented in D. Smith, 'New Movements in the Sociology of Youth', *British Journal of Sociology*, Vol. 32, No. 2, 1981.
7. J.C. Coleman, *The Nature of Adolescence*, Methuen, 1980; J. Adelson (ed.), *Handbook of Adolescent Psychology*, Wiley, 1980. J.J. Conger and A.C. Peterson, *Adolescence and Youth*, 3rd edition, Harper & Row, 1984.
8. D. Marsland (ed.), *Education and Youth*, Falmer Press, 1987.
9. D. Marsland, 'On Education: Vast Horizons, Meagre Visions', in D.C. Anderson et al., *Breaking the Spell of the Welfare State*, Social Affairs Unit, 1981.
10. D. O'Keeffe, 'Labour in Vain: Truancy, Industry, and the School Curriculum', in A. Flew et al., *The Pied Pipers of Education*, Social Affairs Unit, 1981.
11. D. Marsland, 'Work to be Done', *Youth Call*, 1984.
12. The Albemarle Report, *The Youth Service in England and Wales*, HMSO, 1960; the Milson-Fairbairn Report, *Youth and Community Work in the 1970s*, HMSO, 1969; the Thompson Report, *Experience and Participation*, HMSO, 1982.
13. E. Mathura, 'Young People and Values', *Education and Youth*, op. cit.
14. On the connections between social arrangements and moral values see R. Segalman and D. Marsland, *Cradle to Grave: Comparative Perspectives on the State of Welfare*, Macmillan/Social Affairs Unit, forthcoming in 1988, and H. Parker, *The Moral Hazards of Social Benefits*, Institute of Economic Affairs, 1982. In relation to the timeliness and political feasibility of such a programme, consider the results of a recent national poll by Audience Selection (reported in the *Daily Telegraph*, 29 January, 1988) which found *as many as 85 per cent* either completely opposed to the use of four letter words on television or prepared to accept it only 'exceptionally' or late at night.
15. D. Marsland, 'Young People, the Family, and the State', in D.C. Anderson and G. Dawson (eds.), *Family Portraits*, Social Affairs Unit, 1986.
16. D. Marsland, 'Trends in Youth Education and Development, East and West', in K. Evans and I. Haffenden (eds.), *International Perspectives on Youth Development*, Croom Helm, 1988. I argue there that the Communist world correctly acknowledges the importance of youth – and grossly misuses this understanding, while the free world fails altogether to recognise how significant the situation and condition of young people is, and to its cost does little therefore to help them positively.
17. D. Marsland, *Issues and Methods in Social Education*, National Youth Bureau, 1988.

18. L. Button, *Developmental Group Work with Adolescents*, Hodder and Stoughton, 1985. Button's important work is examined in detail in D. Marsland and M. Day, 'Capitalizing on Youth: Group Work in Education', in *Education and Youth*, op. cit.
19. E. Erikson, *Childhood and Society*, Triad/Paladin, 1977.
20. For a fuller account of the essential role of social education in the positive development of young people see D. Marsland, *Issues and Methods...*, op. cit.

6 Children's Nutrition: Progress and Problems

Barbara Pickard

1 Summary and Introduction

It is paradoxical that as a wider range of food has become available so the task of ensuring children receive an appropriate diet has become more controversial. This is partly because the greater variety of food has allowed greater scope to the faddists.

The faddists are interested in the unusual – hyperactivity and so-called allergy. They are also obsessed by the problem of obese middle-aged men. None of this is much help to the normal child. He or she simply needs a balanced diet with some food from each of the main food groups – meat, fish, eggs, pulses and nuts form one group; bread and cereals, including oats, rice and pasta comprise the second; milk and dairy produce the third; and fresh vegetables and fruit the fourth. Indeed, inflicting faddist obsessions on children can be dangerous. Children need food not only to supply energy for the very active lives they often lead, but also for growth and development. On a bulky, high fibre diet, children's limited stomach capacity can make them feel full before they have eaten the calories they require and there is an additional danger that they may not obtain sufficient quality or quantity of the protein and minerals they require.

More education about food is desirable but if parents really want to ensure their children are eating properly there is perhaps no better way than for them all to sit down to meals together, a habit which is unfortunately far less common than it used to be.

2 The wider the availability of food, the greater the problem of what to eat

'For your child, eating can be a wonderful adventure' says an old

78

leaflet but today's interested parent is pretty unlikely to consider fun, wonder or enjoyment when it comes to the question of food for little John or Sarah. The serious pursuit of the ultimate healthy diet is a war waged against 'junk' food and a struggle to avoid allergy, hyperactivity, vitamin and mineral deficiencies and even premature thickening of the arteries.

These kinds of problems trouble many parents, despite the fact that there is a greater availability and a wider choice of food than ever before. Why this paradox? Is it because our relative national affluence in both the global context and in terms of the historical perspective, removes the worry about getting *enough* to eat but allows us to replace it with anxiety over exactly *what* to eat? Certainly the continual airing of controversial issues about nutrition by the media prompts more and more parents to become concerned. Perhaps, too, the uncertainty engendered by shifting social barriers relating to woman's position in society has not been conducive to stability of thought and action on the domestic front. Women at home feel guilty because they are not out working, whilst working women feel guilty because they are not at home more with the children.

Whilst many parents are unduly worried about their children's diets, lack of parental guidance about nutrition is the plight of other children; for them, the breakdown in traditional family meal patterns and substitution of staple foods by energy-rich but nutrient-poor snacks, has created new problems of malnutrition. This chapter will address itself to some of the current dietary issues which relate to children, but it is pertinent first to place such issues in the context of the progress which has been made in the last 100 years or so.

3   Gains in knowledge about nutrition in danger of being sacrificed to the faddists

In 1850, out of every 1000 babies born alive, approximately 150 would die in their first year and 40 out of every 1000 among one to four year olds would also die. By 1950 these death rates had fallen dramatically (to around 30 per 1000 for infants under one year old and one per 1000 for children aged one to four) and have continued their downward trend since then. Two of the most important factors contributing to these declines in the death rate were better living conditions and improved nutrition. Today it is from the most extreme examples in the developing countries that we see how poor diets can take their toll, especially on the young. Severe malnutrition not only hinders growth and development but also increases susceptibility to infectious diseases. Infection then aggravates the malnutrition, for example by loss of appetite and/or diarrhoea. In this country in the nineteenth century, the malnutrition of extreme poverty acted in a similar way, but as the quantity and quality of food improved there was a gradual and sustained increase in the level of general health.

By the turn of the century, children were much less likely to die than they were a century before, but gradually it became apparent that, despite the progress, all was not well. In 1934 over half of the young men who went to army recruiting offices did not come up to the required physical standards, and surveys in schools showed many children were malnourished. Not only were the poorer members of society showing physical signs of inadequate nutrition, but they were also more likely to suffer from disease and premature death than the affluent. In 1936 Lord Boyd Orr organised detailed surveys of the diets of families in different social classes. The results showed that many poor people were going hungry, with a 30 per cent shortfall in calories and great disparities between the lower and higher income groups in purchases of the more expensive foods such as milk, butter, eggs, meat, fish, fruit and vegetables other than potatoes.

Over the same period, in the backwaters of learned institutions, diligent scientists had quietly been unravelling some of food's hitherto hidden complexities. The importance to good health of vitamins and minerals and of high quality protein began to be recognised. The very foods which were most expensive and hence least available to the poor were those which came to be regarded as the most nutritious. It is no wonder then that when all manner of welfare schemes were introduced to encourage an improvement in the nation's nutrition, emphasis was placed on dairy products, meat, eggs and fish as well as on fruit and vegetables. The beneficial effects of such schemes were gradually to be seen in children's improved growth and health.

Today that emphasis has changed; more attention is focussed on the prevention of heart disease in middle-aged men than on rearing healthy children. There are obsessions with slimming diets and with food to avoid rather than what is good. The pendulum may have swung too far; we are beset with a plague of ill-informed food faddists, and vulnerable groups such as children need protection from the kind of restrictive advice appropriate only for sedentary over-indulgent middle-aged men.

4 Children's nutritional needs different from adults?

A new term has crept into the vernacular – 'muesli-belt malnutrition'. Among other uses, it describes the problem occasionally seen in children whose failure to thrive is not attributable to poverty or to poor standards of education. On the contrary, it is characteristic of the more affluent and educated classes and is probably a consequence of the 'little bit of knowledge is a dangerous thing' syndrome.

It is unfortunate that the fashion for all things fibrous and against foods of animal origin was taken up quite so avidly by well-meaning parents. Their children's diets were probably already satisfactory and it is feared that some parents may have made detrimental changes. One such change is the unenlightened adoption of a vegetarian diet. Of course, large numbers of people are just as healthy on vegetarian diets as those eating more varied foods. However, if the choice of foods is not wise, there are potential problems, especially for children. These stem from the fact that children's needs for calories and for specific nutrients are greater, relative to their body size, than for adults. They need food not only to supply energy for the very active lives they often lead, but also for growth and development. On a bulky, high fibre diet, the limited stomach capacity of children can make them feel full before they have eaten the calories they require. In some cases, there is also a danger that a young child may not obtain sufficient quantity and/or quality of protein. Finally, a high intake of fibre has the potential to inhibit the absorption of minerals. Since minerals such as iron, zinc and calcium are already less readily absorbed from foods of plant origin than from animal sources, any further limitation of availability by excess fibre is obviously not desirable.

Even more harm could be done if the current passion for all that is low fat is extended to the young. Nutritionists, dietitians and paediatricians have expressed their concern about low-fat diets for children and the idea that young children should be given skimmed rather than whole milk. Even the bible of the anti-fat lobby, the COMA report, stated quite clearly that its recommendations were 'not intended for infants, or for children below the age of five who usually obtain a substantial proportion of dietary energy from cow's milk'. Skimmed milk has no fat-soluble vitamins and only half of the energy content of whole milk. Surveys in the United States showed that infants fed skimmed milk did not grow as well as infants given whole milk, and the body's reserves of fat began to be depleted. In view of the general consensus that it is better, in terms of brain development, for a child to be slightly over-nourished than under-nourished in the early years, it is essential that unwitting parents be given more accurate information on which to make their family food choices.

5   Breast feeding best for majority of babies

By 1960 the practice of breastfeeding had declined so much that the United Kingdom could be termed a bottlefeeding nation. Around this time, however, a counter-trend began to develop, although the reasons for this are not fully understood. Was it the growth of women's self-help organisations such as the National Childbirth Trust and La Leche League, the general reaction against modern technology, or the growing awareness of the true extent of the differences between breastmilk and formula milks – not just in nutritional terms but in anti-allergic, anti-infective and other beneficial properties? Or was it a combination of these, together with a renewed emphasis on breastfeeding by health professionals?

By 1980, two thirds of mothers in England and Wales breastfed initially, although as expected the highest incidence was among mothers in the upper socio-economic groups and over a third of mothers stopped breastfeeding within six weeks of the birth. Why is breastfeeding not more popular, when the gurus of breastfeeding present such powerful arguments that breastfed babies are healthier, their growth rate is better, they suffer fewer infections, fewer allergic diseases and are less likely to suffer from some of the diseases of later life?

Possibly the greatest disincentive to breastfeeding is the notion that the mother has insufficient milk. This particular difficulty is almost exclusive to the developed countries and in most cases it is the anxiety which is the problem rather than any fundamental anatomical or physiological defect. Anxiety is a potent inhibitor of the milk let-down reflex; the baby cannot obtain milk already in the breast unless there is 'let-down'. Another bone of contention about which some health visitors and midwives despair, is the ardent determination to breastfeed of reed-like mothers who are unwilling to eat well and hence unable to meet the optimum needs of their child. Yet almost all these problems could be overcome by perseverance and patience together with the help and support of others such as health professionals and self-help groups.

For mothers, there are pros and cons to breastfeeding; as far as the vast majority of babies are concerned, breastfeeding is the only way and anything less is inferior. Unfortunately, any slogan along these lines would suffer an early demise – it is not done to make people feel guilty, even if by condoning their actions, we condemn their children to second-best. Nevertheless, there must be cautious optimism for the eventual return of breastfeeding to its proper status.

6   Inadequate nutrition: the role of money, fashion and education

Today overt malnutrition from sheer lack of food is not common in this country. However, children getting enough calories can still be malnourished because they may be less likely to get their energy from items such as meat, cheese and fish and far more likely to consume chocolates, crisps and cola. Problems of malnutrition are more severe in the lower socio-economic groups and children may be affected throughout their development from womb to adolescence.

A detailed study of the diet of poor pregnant women in Hackney compared to women in Hampstead showed how poverty compromised the health of the young infant. Diets poor both in quality and quantity were associated with a greater risk of low birth weight and all its consequent disadvantages. Another at risk stage occurs following weaning of toddlers from fortified commercial babyfoods. A survey of infants from socially deprived areas by the Early Childhood Development Centre in Bristol, revealed a disturbing and sudden relative decline in the intake of many essential nutrients at this time.

For older children, the picture appears to be rosier. A recent DHSS survey of school children from all social groups concluded energy intakes were adequate and the intake of other nutrients was on 'average' above the Recommended Daily Allowance (RDA). The cult of the 'average' can be dangerous however; it engenders complacency and malnutrition is after all a problem of individuals and not of 'average' children. It may be misleading too to trust the infallibility of the RDA. The average daily intake of vitamin C, for example, was 49mg and well above the RDA (25mg) but a glance at the *range* of intake shows almost a quarter of children consumed less than the RDA. Whilst 25mg vitamin C per day (available from one good helping of spring cabbage or half an orange) may prevent scurvy, many would deny its adequacy for optimum health, and if 60mg were taken as a more realistic target, then three-quarters of the children surveyed had intakes less than this.

The diets of the majority of schoolgirls were deficient in iron, calcium and riboflavin. This is hardly surprising in view of the penchant for young girls to follow fashion and the trend to emulate those irresponsible fanatics who condemn the very foods which are good sources of these missing nutrients, namely meat and dairy produce. The detrimental effects of such deficiencies may not show today but in years to come will become manifest, perhaps as anaemia, osteoporosis or other disorders linked to poor health.

It can be argued that the major deficiency, as far as malnutrition and poverty is concerned, is one of money, and when rent and other expenses have been paid, there is little left for food. Yet even financial restraints are only partly responsible. There is a dearth of knowledge about economical choice of foods and how best to prepare them; there is also often a lack of access to basic kitchen facilities. It is only the select few, among the educated poor, who can appreciate that baked beans on toast with egg and cabbage is a nut-ritional luxury compared to inferior but costly soft drinks and snack biscuits. As in earlier years, improvements in diet depend upon improvements in education and general social conditions.

7 Food allergy not as widespread as simplistic diagnoses imply

Food allergy is an emotive subject; it has been dismissed by some as quackery and by others sublimely accepted as something which adversely affects most if not all of us. The truth probably lies some-where in the middle. Strictly speaking, food *allergy* is an adverse reaction to food which involves the immune or defence system of the body. Susceptible individuals usually respond to the common staple foods of a particular culture, for example cow's milk, eggs and wheat-based foods in this country. In other countries different foods will top the list and the order of foods in the allergy 'league table' can also change if dietary habits change. For example, as soy protein has become more widely used in this country, allergy to soy has moved up the league table; a fact not well known by devotees of soy who strongly advocate it for allergy-susceptible children.

Other unpleasant responses to food are generally classified as food *intolerances*: these include biochemical deficiencies such as the inability to digest lactose in milk, pharmacological reactions to compounds in such foods as cheese, chocolate and red wine; and psychologically-based food aversion (this is quite common and unfavourable physical symptoms occur only when the patient is aware of having eaten a suspect food, not when the food is dis-guised). There is also the 'do-it-yourself' misdiagnosis of food allergy by enthusiastic parents who may impose rigid and very limited diets on their children. These may be unnecessary as well as anti-social and could be potentially harmful. Very restricted diets can lead to malnutrition and malnutrition itself can predispose towards food intolerance, so there is a real risk of a downward spiral in the child's health.

Although children are more likely to suffer from food intoler-ance than adults, many will grow out of the condition. Estimates of incidence vary widely, partly because many of the symptoms are not exclusive to food allergy and partly because of the difficulty of accurate diagnosis. Many diagnostic methods leave much to be desired and one survey revealed numerous discrepancies when duplicate samples were sent to several different clinics. Perhaps the major beneficiaries of private allergy-testing centres are those who run them.

The most accurate technique is the long drawn-out one of an exclusion diet, together with subsequent double-blind food challenge. (The suspect food is disguised, then presented or omitted at random from test meals; only later is the labelling 'code' broken and patient and doctor informed whether or not the suspect food has been consumed.) In this way, a physiological reaction to food can be distinguished from a psychological one and treatment planned accordingly. These methods are costly, very time-consuming and involve an enormous amount of commitment by parents, children, and health professionals. For the truly allergic child, however, they are well worth the trouble and effort involved.

8   No simple link between diet and hyperactivity

Another subject awash with scepticism is hyperactivity in children. As with allergy, accurate diagnosis can be difficult, the causes are not fully understood and methods of treatment are even more controversial. Many parents and some doctors have followed the recommendations of Dr Ben Feingold, who formulated a special exclusion diet for hyperactive American children, but the results of double-blind trials testing the diet have shown mainly negative results and have tended to reinforce the establishment's misgivings.

Developments at grass roots level have been quite different. Following the successful use of the diet for her six-year-old hyperactive son, Sally Bunday, working voluntarily with Irene Colquhoun, set up the Hyperactive Children's Support Group (HACSG). Thousands of desperate parents wrote for advice and are still writing; these two women, with no qualifications but a grim determination to learn, can be credited with markedly advancing the cause of hyperactive children in this country. Their pleas for support from the government were ignored and the establishment has been predictably ultra-cautious but, regardless of scientific proof either one way or the other, the manufacturers' response to public pressure has been to cut down on artificial additive use. 'Additive-free' has become the latest selling-point. There are benefits from this consumer-led revolution, including the cutback on the extravagant usage of cosmetic and nutritionally unnecessary additives, but there are potential dangers, including the risk of food poisoning if preservatives and other functional additives are omitted from packaged foods and parents fail to follow new storage/handling recommendations.

The increased public awareness of hyperactivity has prompted more research into the condition. One recent carefully planned study of severely hyperactive children noted that 62 out of 76 children improved on some kind of special diet; the commonest substances evoking reactions were benzoic acid and tartrazine, although no child reacted to these alone; foods provoking a response included those commonly associated with allergy, such as milk, wheat, eggs, chocolate and oranges. Other factors were obviously involved and children from families with psychological problems did not improve quite so well. When the diet was continued, some children gradually ceased to react to certain foods. This might suggest that an improvement in the nutritional status of the children could also play a part in reducing the tendency to hyperactivity. The practical recommendations of the HACSG suggest avoidance of many additive-containing foods but, by the same token, they advocate increased consumption of less highly processed and more nutritious foods; a child on such a diet will not only receive fewer additives but will also improve his nutrient intake.

Further progress in understanding this condition could be made if there were greater co-operation and communication between the self-help groups and the establishment. The public could learn and understand why scientists are so reticent and why they abhor unscrupulous entrepreneurs cashing in on the layperson's ignorance; the medical and scientific professions could learn a great deal from parents about the problems and practicalities of caring for hyperactive children.

9   Whatever the latest dietary fashion, children's needs have not changed

One cannot help feeling that somewhere along the road of progress, the focus of attention has drifted away from the nurture of the normal child into the mire of controversy about specialised conditions. Yet the needs of the majority of children have not changed and, though they may be difficult for some to have access to, they are pretty simple – a stable, secure and safe environment, with good food and plenty of fresh air and exercise. We can reach the moon but many people would be hard-pressed to define exactly what is 'good' food for children. It is another example of our modern tendency to dissect the tree instead of observe the forest.

The observers of yesteryear had the answer and in the 1930s they were quite definite. Sir Robert McCarrison stated 'the greatest single factor in the acquisition and maintenance of good health is perfectly constituted food'. Clara Davis found that newly weaned babies and young children, if left to themselves, could choose a balanced healthy diet and thrive on it, providing only basic simple foodstuffs were offered – no highly processed foods were included in the experiment. Although the diets of these children varied enormously from day to day and from child to child, they were all found to be well-balanced when assessed over the course of a few weeks. The constraints and social customs of today make it impracticable if not impossible to repeat the exercise in households around the land, but there is a lesson to be learned. Davis wrote in 1934 'These babies and young children ate much more fruit, meat, eggs and fat than paediatricians commonly advise or than the average child ever has the chance to eat, and less of the cereals and green leafy vegetables about which we hear so much these days'. Things have not changed much.

10   A varied and well-balanced diet – 'functional and fun'

Whilst acknowledging that a good diet is the foundation but not the whole framework for good health, parents can take positive steps to make available a variety of simple foods to form the basis of their children's needs. The variety need not involve great cost or effort;

one simple way is to choose foods from each of four main food groups; meat, fish, eggs, pulses and nuts form one group; bread and cereals including oats, rice and pasta comprise the second; milk and dairy produce the third; and fresh vegetables and fruit the fourth. Parents and children can also sit together as families around the kitchen or dining table as often as is possible; this social custom is slowly dying and leaving a trail of problems behind it. Those same parents can then sit back and be a bit more tolerant and philosophical about the surplus items in their children's diets; the sweets, crisps and soft drinks. For the majority, these items are not the deadly villains they are made out to be, as long as they remain as occasional extras to the basic diet rather than forming a major part of it.

Fortunately today, there are still experts in nutrition who are also equipped with common sense and breadth of vision. The nutritionist Dr. Michael Gibney sees the true pursuit of health involving an outlook on diet which sees food as gastronomically pleasing and mentally and physically invigorating. In his view, food should be seen not as medicine and not just as fuel, but as both functional and fun. Perhaps the old leaflet for parents about food for their children was not so wrong after all.

7 The Needs of Children Revisited

Richard Whitfield

1 Summary and Introduction

The standards of child rearing and child care in our society are frequently inadequate when assessed against the yardstick of what we now know that children need in order to thrive – biologically, socially, emotionally, intellectually and spiritually. While there are many structural forces undermining children's best interests, there is also widespread igorance of children's developmental needs so that parents' decisions about the context and practice of their child rearing are frequently less sensitive and coherent than they might be. For many children the world becomes a more confusing environment than it need be; the products of this include alienation, disruptive or withdrawn social behaviour, poor social relationships and diminished educational achievement.

Nurturing the next generation is *the* most important human activity of any culture if society is to be maintained and extended. Society is giving less time, attention, resources, status to, and education about the field of child rearing than it should. The site for most child rearing is and will remain the home and family. There, committed parenthood (or its obverse) are enacted day by day with profound influences on the child. Committed parenthood should provide:

- Love – not in a vague sense or feeling, but in the sense of will and commitment to care for children regardless of their appearance, personality or attitudes and with a care which responds to their differences. Such love also involves correction and restraint.
- Security – especially in the relationship of the parents.
- A basis in education and new experience.

90

- Encouragement and the development of responsibility.

This chapter outlines the key research-based conditions for optimum child development. These require us to reconsider and change practices and policies which, regrettably, have become culturally acceptable in our essentially adult-orientated world. For example, children's interests are rarely, if ever, best served if:

- they lack two viable parents, one of each sex, who are committed to them and to each other legally and psychologically;
- if they become separated from one or both of their parents for lengthy periods during their upbringing;
- if their parents divorce, the family home is disturbed and a range of surrogate or actual step-parent figures are introduced;
- if both their parents participate in paid employment on a full-time basis external to the home at any stage in their development towards adulthood, unless a nearby member of the extended family or neighbour can compensate (for example by providing a welcome at home when children and adolescents return from school); or
- if parental lifestyles in these or other ways do not consider children's needs as paramount, thereby directing insufficient personal availability, energy and attention towards child rearing tasks; most substitute parental care is both costly and has psychological and practical limitations.

These examples are by no means inherently sexist. They simply emphasise the joint responsibilities of mothers with fathers to endeavour to constrain their freedom, though by no means to starve their own needs, as they co-parent. In most cases in our culture it requires fathers to become more involved in child rearing and domestic life.

2   Perfect parenting difficult to achieve so adequate standards must be sought

Those who endeavour to be conscientious and caring parents find the parenthood role demanding. Like life itself, parenthood combines joy and disappointment, pleasure and pain, success and failure. Fundamentally, it is akin to full-time work with, for most of us, only occasional time off during the first two decades of each child's life, and even that takes much organising and the willingness of others to substitute. If our children are to thrive and achieve something close to their full potentials, parenthood needs to be recognised as a vocation requiring *time*, care, status and resources.

However, almost all of us embark on parenthood with little or no preparation. With the decline of large families, and therefore less sibling care, for many of us the first baby we really meet is the one we have. Yet the most important activity in any culture is the nurturing of the next generation. Despite eleventh hour optional prenatal classes, this general unpreparedness is as unjustified as it is surprising, particularly in view of the wide range of knowledge which we now have about the optimum conditions for child growth and development. Furthermore, during a period of social change more rapid than at any previous phase of recorded history, sensitive parenthood is probably at its most demanding.

Our efforts to provide for and to understand our children also go beyond their immediate generation, since they, all too swiftly, become tomorrow's parents. Patterns and models of parenthood have a tendency to 'visit to the fourth generation'. Today's child care significantly conditions the health of marriages and the care of offspring of those unions in the first two or three decades of the next century.

Likewise, understanding of our own temperaments and 'natural' behaviour as spouses and parents is frequently enhanced by retrospective reflection upon the qualities of our own nurturing experience when we were children. Not for one of us will that experience have been perfect, as environmental constraints, stress, impatience, lack of knowledge, and even our own infantile irritability, prompted occasional insensitivity, or worse, thus depriving us of at least some of our inherent and legitimate 'needs' as children. Perfect parenting is both an impossibility and a noxious concept, for nowhere can this life promise unending nurture and unblemished relationships. Hence concern must be with 'good enough' parenting.[1]

3 Four essential needs for rearing healthy and well-balanced children

In 1974–75 an important book[2] about children's needs was prepared for the DHSS by the late Dr. Mia Kellmer Pringle, the founding Director of the National Children's Bureau. It was commissioned by Sir Keith Joseph (who was at that time Secretary of State for Social Services), along with two related publications about parenthood.[3]

Sir Keith at that stage was properly concerned about the so-called 'cycle of deprivation' which appeared to be persisting for many children despite the continuing development of the health, education and social services. In the preface to the book he noted that child welfare was essentially a matter of harmonising efforts to alleviate material deprivation, notably poverty and poor housing, with 'a wider understanding of the emotional needs of children and of the importance from the earliest years of the quality of relationships between a child and those responsible for his care.' Dr. Pringle's book which drew extensively upon interdisciplinary research findings of human development, remains an important benchmark for improvements to child welfare in Britain. Its principles are too often ignored in both public policy and private practice, yet they stand the test of time.

In summary, given the absence of obvious physical handicaps in the child, a sound diet, appropriate clothing and sufficient sleep, the optimum development of children depends upon the following four environmental conditions or 'needs' being met: the need for reliable love from and secure attachment to parent figures, reflecting that 'psychological' rather than biological parenthood is crucial; the need for new experiences which gradually extend the child's world; these, when explained by patient teaching, in home and school, enable the child to develop structures of meaning and understanding so that the world is experienced more in terms of order than chaos; the need for praise, recognition and affirmation, reflecting the fact that secure identities are jeopardised by overly critical and negative environments; and the need to be given responsibilities appropriate to the child's level of development, which is again a reflection of the confirmation of identity through the exercise of constructive social roles.

Even though there remains some concern about children's diets and their physical fitness (for the two car family, increases in TV viewing, and the decline of exacting physical education programmes in schools have caused many youngsters to take insufficient exercise), it is these distinctively human needs which this chapter addresses. We have not yet taken sufficiently seriously the emotional, moral and social needs of children which are the foundation for their intellectual and educational functioning, and their growth in personal autonomy and responsibility which characterise sound citizenship.

4   Parental commitment essential element of child rearing

From our knowledge of conception onwards the most natural people to provide the love that the child needs are we, the parents. Every child is entitled to dependable and loving relationships with two parents, one of each sex, or equivalent permanent substitutes such as adoptive parents. Through the supportive attention of two complementary parents children come to establish a sense of their own worth, identity and sexuality. Lone parenthood, whether caused by death, divorce or design, is inherently more demanding, and generally a more risky venture for both parent and child, if only because of the usually more limited overall resources of the single carer.

The crucial characteristic of mature parental love is that it envelops our children in good times and bad. We love our children regardless of their appearance, personality or abilities; we love them when their behaviour is unlovable and irritating, while to take the time and trouble to correct anti-social behaviour during the years of growing up is an important aspect of helping them to learn about boundaries in the social and physical world.

As loving parents we are willing to take, and to go on taking trouble with our children. Indeed, parental love may be viewed as our continuing willingness to extend ourselves in order to foster our children's social, educational, emotional and spiritual growth. This emphasises that our love is far more a matter of *will* and *commitment* rather than feeling; indeed love based mainly upon emotion is a poor foundation for all human relationships.[4]

The parental love which our children need involves courage, a willingness to attend and to listen as well as to explain. It involves judicious giving and judicious withholding. It recognises the individuality and separateness of the child, and it guards against possessiveness and over-dependency which can perpetuate essentially infantile attitudes into later phases of life.

Reflective and emotionally sensitive fathers are only rare products of male socialisation in our society, but Laurie Lee's musings after the birth of his first (and only) child captures much of the fundamental essence of concerned parenthood:

> This girl then, my child, this parcel of will and warmth, began to fill the cottage with her obsessive purpose...
>
> I'd been handed twenty odd years wrapped up in this bundle, and hoped to see her grow, learn to totter, to run into the garden, run back, and call this place home. But I realised from these beginnings that I'd got a daughter whose life was already separate from mine, whose will already followed its own directions, and who was quickly correcting my woolly preconceptions of her by being something quite different. She was a child of herself and would be what she was. I was merely the keeper of her temporary helplessness.[5]

But being a loving 'keeper' is an active and working role in which we are cast both as providers and catalysts in the processes of our children's becoming. We soon learn that this involves some sacrifice of our adult freedoms, for example over night feeding, our social life, holiday arrangements, and so on. Yet children's perceptions of parental commitment, long suffering and sacrifice as they mature is an important element in the adult confirmation for them of parental love. In few other relationships do children have the opportunity of experiencing what it is like to be cared for without conditions, while such experience will become foundation material for their own later work as lovers and parents.

We must not however confuse parental love, sometimes expressed as sacrifice, with parental masochism. Parents are people too. They have needs for nurture, healing[6] and personal growth which, if ignored by round-the-clock servitude to their families, eventually undermines the ability to be an effective psychological parent. Spending some time extending oneself as a mother or father for one's own personal and spiritual growth is essential if we are to sustain a vibrant love for others. Dedicated parents often unwisely ignore this during the busy years of child rearing, though time, resources and opportunities for parental growth are too much at a premium in our society.[7]

5 Duty of parents to provide secure framework for children's development

Our children's need for security is met first and foremost by a stable framework among our family relationships; such stability will in general help us to reflect consistent attitudes and to behave dependably. Also important, especially for young children, are the security of a familiar place, familiar objects and of a familiar routine. Development in childhood is necessarily about change and exploration, some of which can be frightening to the child, whether in toddlerhood, or adolescence. Hence a predictable background environment gives continuity, and it encourages safer exploration by the child of its own frontiers.

In terms of practical consequences, our children's need for security, given that we as individual parents love them, is likely to be met through warm and supportive marital relationships, not moving house and home more than proves essential, and developing a domestic routine which has more pattern than chaos. It is important that when inevitable variations occur in life's pattern they are explicable, for a child's security is undermined by excessive randomness.

There has perhaps been a tendency to emphasise too exclusively good parent-child relationships for fostering security, while ignoring the parent-parent relationship which the child observes and which can be a powerful model for developing its own relations in the wider world. While parental and marriage relationships, like all others, are rarely static, the level of confidence that each partner holds for the other conditions the climate for child rearing. Insecure parents in insecure marriages tend to create insecure home environments for their children. Hence, the sensitive enrichment of our parental and marriage relationships[8] is essential if we are to develop our optimum child care practice. As we work at our marriages with all their problematic intensities (often related to our own wider experience), we work both for our own and our children's security.

Above all, stable and secure family life provides children with a sense of personal continuity. Knowledge of and reminders (such as photographs) of the past help us to both make sense of the present and to give hope for a future in which the necessary risks of being alive can be assimilated without trauma. Secure attachment to new people, concerns and places outside the immediate family circle are of course a necessary part of that future hope.

6 Home: the most important source of children's education

New experiences, provided they can be meaningfully related to what has gone before, enlarge the human personality. The child's growth as a person, rather than simply as a body, is dependent upon a gradual exploration of the physical and social environment. Such exploration, based initially upon the child's natural curiosity, requires stimulation (but not over-stimulation), guidance and explanation (but not excessive control and didactic lecturing) from parents and other carers.

From the very early days of life children's educational capabilities, that is their responsiveness to the varied growth tasks which teaching and learning in their widest sense open up to them, are being determined. The emotional and cultural climate of the home is fundamental to the provision of safe and valuable new experiences throughout childhood; these are extended by organised pre-school experience and, later, by the formal educational system. Given appropriate explanation by careful teaching, our children's gradually extending experience becomes organised and differentiated so that distinctive forms of meaning and reasoning become apparent to their developing intellects. Children begin to learn that different language and procedural 'rules' apply to thinking and action in mathematics, science, the arts, history, religion, and so on.

Fundamentally, the formal educational system exists because

there are inevitable limitations to the specialist functions of the home as educator in extending children's understanding and experiences of the world, and in providing them with an array of useful skills to enable them to participate in our complex society. But the school and college systems can only build upon what children and students bring to the classroom from their prior experience, most of which, in terms of time, is derived from home and neighbourhood. Home, school and community are thus interdependent agents for providing children with comprehendable and worthwhile new experiences.[9]

The main specific and irremovable educational functions of the home are concerned with: the development of language-listening, talking and, later, writing; the encouragement of learning through active play; in this the manipulation of toys, body control, sound expressiveness, role play, and make-believe each contribute to child development; the fostering of social and relationships skills partly by modelling; and, developing an awareness and understanding of the moral order.

Each of these facets is inter-dependent, while language is the key to effective communication, to making new experiences intelligible and to understanding different forms of reasoning. The language of the home is a part of its climate; it mediates between thought, emotion and behaviour; it links new experience with the familiar; and, as parents, we have no little control upon the ways in which it is used to foster our children's growth.

7 Parents should provide incentives for children to realise their potential

To grow from being a helpless baby into a self-reliant adult, and to be sustained at each stage of that complex and uneven process, requires strong incentives. The will to thrive, and the spirit to stay fully alive are destructable by environmental circumstances. Each of us has the potential for immense psychological strength, but also for delicate vulnerability or destructiveness.

Centrally, from our very earliest days, we gain the incentive to go on growing from the recognition, praise and affirmation given to us principally by those to whom we are psychologically attached. If those who love us show pleasure at our success, and give us praise, we are affirmed, and our developing identity is thereby confirmed. One of our basic propensities is to wish to please those who love us, provided of course we perceive that their expectations of our behaviour are reasonable and sensitive in relation to our innate nature and stage of development. Inappropriate expectations can make us feel angry, frustrated, and even rejected and unloved, which alone gives us reason as parents to endeavour to understand as much as we can about norms and variations in child development.

Of course much human learning from cradle onwards is a matter of trial and error. We and our children can and do learn from our mistakes. Sometimes our errors become clear to us without anyone else intervening to point them out. At other times we are blind or slow to catch on to our failures; on these occasions we need clear correction and explanation from those around us if we are to inhabit the real world. The form in which we are corrected, particularly by those who are close to us, is however important to the maintenance of our sense of well-being. Children, and even adults, may become anxious and fearful of making mistakes for fear of personal punitive correction by 'superiors'; this can imply not only that error or misunderstanding is being corrected, but also that the personal identity is being demeaned.

There is clearly a balance to be struck between creating a climate which is excessively and unrealistically full of either praise, and possibly bogus affirmation, or of correction and criticism. Genuine, reasonable and consistent encouragement to move forward, involving 'permission' to err, is what we all need to sustain our spirits, whether as children or parents.

8 Parents should balance supportive role with children's need to develop independence

This final prime need of our children is associated both with their sense of importance and the acquisition of tangible contributing roles in the social world, and with their moral development. A sense of responsibility, whether to oneself or to others, is essentially an ethical notion involving perception and understanding of the boundaries and interactions between the self and the rest of the world.

We meet our children's need for responsibility by encouraging their personal independence at a pace which they can assimilate without becoming confused, frustrated, or simply lonely. The 'let me do it' urge and the 'please help me' plaint jostle together throughout life, but it is in childhood that we begin to learn about the changing boundaries of our dependence and independence.

As parents we need progressively to encourage our children to be responsible for their possessions, such as toys and clothes, but also including their bodies. With regard to the latter, we have an important role in the personal health education of our children, including the sexual components, in partnership with schools. As our youngsters reach adolescence we will wisely recognise that their developing sense of responsibility in these and other matters (such as peer group participation) must diminish our parental rights to control; incrementally we need to change our parental role to that of friendly adviser.

The fostering of our children's independence and responsibility is a delicate balancing act for most of us, for our love urges both their protection from harm and their freedom to be. We must give our youngsters roots, but also wings. The parental duty to advise, to give reasoned viewpoint and opinion is however crucial at every stage of development if we are to sustain genuine relationships with our offspring. For the most part, if we have been 'good enough' parents, our children will want to know what we think, and what our cumulative wisdom might suggest, especially at times when they are in or feel in 'tight corners'.

It is now known that moral development procedes through a number of inter-related stages,[10] eventually characterised by an ability to act according to our own conscience and principles, duly considering within our actions the rights and feelings of others. Such moral autonomy and 'inner direction' is only achieved if from early childhood we have learned about boundaries to the self and of the likely consequences of our actions upon others.

The framework of social discipline in the home is crucial in laying foundations for moral action and responsible behaviour. Wisely, this will progress from accepting very young children behaving to obtain what they need in a relatively egocentric manner, through to a phase of conformity in which there is respect for rules (including rewards and punishments) which are imposed by parents, and teachers, as authority figures. This 'outer directioning' of youngsters, by social rules not of their own making is an essential stepping stone to their later achievement of inner direction, this transition to mature moral insight always being assisted by reasoned and reasonable parental discipline. This, no less than keeping our children fed and clothed, requires parental effort and sensitivity, and is a crucial manifestation of our love for them.

9 Parents should respond to children's changing needs as they develop

This somewhat daunting array of basic children's needs is however only the 'warp' of the cloth which sensitive parenthood must create. The 'weft' is provided by a framework of time sequenced, inter-dependent and interactive phases of child development. There is general agreement about the nature of these phases (Table 1), though there are marked individual variations, even in the same family, regarding the pace and extent of each phase; the chronological ages shown are therefore only an appropriate guideline.

Each of these phases is characterised by clusters of physical, intellectual and social traits which give indications of the kinds of active parental and other caregiver responses which are likely to facilitate further development. But similar cues at different ages and with different children need differing interpretations. For example, exaggerated 'bragging' behaviour at four represents reality testing and the deciphering of the 'rules' of the social environment; at twelve it more likely reflects underlying feelings of social inadequacy. Temperament and personality variations also lead to varied signs which require individual understanding. Each of our children is different and there are no unfailing recipes. In terms of an 'aide memoir' of principles, Mia Pringle's 'ten child care commandments' are hard to improve, and reflect much of what this chapter has so far addressed.[11]

So the task of parents is to be major, but not the only providers of their offspring's needs through each developmental phase. The

Table 1: Phases of child development

Stage	Age guideline	Main psychosocial characteristics	Main parenthood functions
Babyhood	−4 to +12 months	Establishment of trust and feelings of essential goodness of the world.	Mother nurture; father support of both. Accept extreme dependency.
Infancy	1 to 3 years	Beginnings of perception of individuality, gender and social boundaries.	Careful management of distance from child. Encourage play, language, walking, safety.
Early childhood	3 to 6 years	Understanding of separateness of self, mother, father, peers. Happy conformity.	Establish generational and role boundaries and social rules. Confirm gender identity.
Late childhood	6 to 12 years	Acceptable periodic separation from parents. Trust of other carers and peers. Make own plans.	Sharing of caring/socialisation with teachers and peers. Encourage variety of interests.
Adolescence	13 to 18 years	Life recapitulation; identity exploration in and beyond home; development of self and differentiation from parents.	Tolerate some regression of youngster, along with new expressions of individuality. Provide advisory service and boundaries to kick against.
Young adulthood	19+ years	Establishment of separate lifestyle and domicile; find adult roles; set up enduring relationships; evaluate worldly abilities.	Accept distance and encourage independence of offspring, accepting them as friendly peers.

phases outlined in Table 1 of course coincide with their parents' natural ageing and complementary phases of their adult development.[12] Family development is thus one of orchestrating ebbs and flows of change in both children and adults. As parents we are gradually required to share the steerage on the bridge of our family vessel with our offspring. It is a complex dynamic, in which a compass and a basic chart can be of enormous help.

10   General principles to which parents should adhere

The general traits which we need for the parental task can be succinctly summarised as:

- a generally consistent outgoing *warmth* towards our children;
- a constant *setting of realistic demands* and expectations of them;
- the *establishment and explanation of a few clear boundaries* for their behaviour, and
- a *preparedness to be flexible* so as to respect the individuality of each child and to maximise the opportunities provided by new experience.

These traits are not unlike those revealed by research into the qualities of effective teachers and counsellors. They are within most peoples' grasp, and we can work to develop them. Parenthood isn't for cowards,[13] but inherently it is not impossibly burdensome, given a few minimally permitting conditions which are partly a matter of public policy.[14]

For the challenge of child rearing almost all of us begin too much as rank amateurs because the knowledge and skills which we ideally need have not been adequately incorporated into our total educational culture. More of us could cope, and cope better, with the varied demands of parenthood if we had better preparation and more extensive ongoing and respectful support.

To use a manufacturing analogy, as parents we are responsible for setting up and monitoring a short 'production run' of a high quality complex 'article' in which prototypes are excluded, mistakes are costly and sometimes irreversible. For many years, it has been my contention, and that of a tiny minority of educators, that parental 'firms' can reduce their risks by acquiring information and understanding about the principles of the 'production process' –

both before the 'production line' is set up, and during the production process itself.

Parenthood and family-related education must now become a national priority if society's properly high expectations of parents are to be socially, morally and politically realistic. At the extremes, the abuse of children in our society is in part a product of cultural indifference regarding the complexities of parenthood. Indeed, the primary prevention of child abuse necessitates sufficient education about parenthood for everyone.[15] Such education, which should not assume that parenthood is for everyone, is required over all the years of schooling, with greater formalisation of studies during adolescence. It requires continuing into adulthood, largely by relaxed community education in which the local and national mass media have a potentially important role to exercise.[16] We have to recognise as a society that meeting the needs of children depends upon meeting the needs of parents.[17] This includes the knowledge and skills necessary to establish and maintain a place of residence; that place which, though it may sometimes change its location, we need to be able to call 'home', as reflected earlier by Laurie Lee.

11   Education for a parental role would benefit all concerned

Here is not the place to elaborate a detailed programme for parenthood-relevant education but the following list of suggested aims and an outline content map convey at least some of the flavour of an adaptable menu.[18]

Some aims for parenthood-related education

- To increase knowledge of the processes of human development from conception to old age.
- To promote an awareness of different ways in which people can and do live together and care for each other, including the framework of marriage.
- To develop and give practice in skills of inter-personal communication and caring.
- To promote an understanding of the inter-relations between life in households and the wider society, including government.

- To increase self knowledge with a view to developing serious attitudes towards life decisions which involve taking responsibility for the care of others; in particular, decisions regarding mating and procreation.
- To increase knowledge of agencies which are available to support the lives of families throughout the life cycle.

In the rudimentary content map (Fig. 2) the specifically parenthood aspects are set within the wider, but concrete, context of home and household establishment, maintenance and management. It will be recognised that the psychosocial aspects of child rearing (on the right of the chart) are linked with many other aspects of domestic concern, providing a potentially exciting variety of educational activities which connect many human concerns and interests.

Within schools such a programme could not only tap pupil motivation; it also provides intellectual challenges for those adolescents who are able to take them up, with formal examination assessment at GCSE and A level in suitable cases. Education for caring is not principally about encouraging empathy; it is much more to do with stretching the intellect and extending the personality than most social skills and human relationships courses have ever recognised. Properly structured, and injected with much needed resources of curriculum and teacher development, it could enrich our most talented university entrants. To date the field remains a low status and under-resourced cottage industry, sadly at great cost to our nation.[20]

12   The pivotal role of parents deserves greater recognition and support

Issues of family formation and parenthood lie at the heart of creating viable societies. We live in an age and culture in which the pace of change in the social fabric is so great that our psychological and sociobiological 'clocks' find it hard to adjust. We as parents are crucial for our children's adaptation to the new environmental conditions. Day-by-day we are at the leading edge of sustaining children's being, and aiding their becoming sufficiently whole to

Fig. 2. Parenthood education in its home context[19]

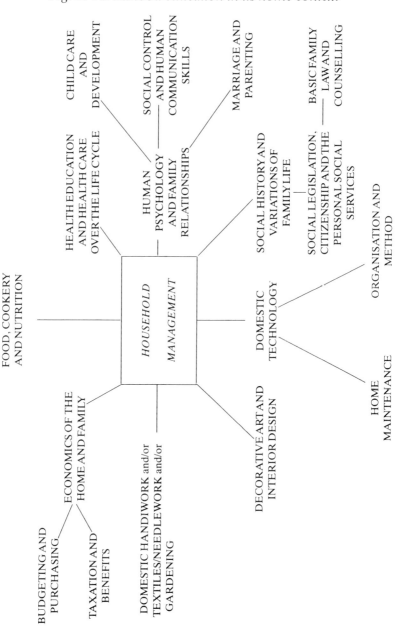

engage meaningfully in the social and economic world. The child rearing work which we do from our home base is of prime value for the society, as well as for our own sense of well-being and satisfaction. When parenting fails in any major respect the emotional and economic costs are often enormous.

Therefore parenthood needs more recognition, resources, status and support in our society. Part of that involves new forms of systematic educational investment for those who are today's or will be tomorrow's parents. A key focus for such preventative educational work must clearly be the developmental needs of children which, having been more systematically illuminated, now set us new, but not impossible standards for 'good enough' parenting. Mia Pringle's ten commandments[21] form a lasting basis for such standards.

Two closing quotations, adapted from Mia Pringle's book which stimulated the title and some of the structure for this chapter, speak, for themselves:

The hallmark of good parenting..... is the single-minded unconditional desire, together with the emotional maturity, to provide a caring home.

Modern parenthood is too demanding and complex a task to be performed well merely because we have all once been children.[22]

Notes and References

1. Interestingly, Dr. Bruno Bettelheim, the internationally renowned veteran child psychiatrist has chosen *A Good Enough Parent* for the title of his latest book, Thames and Hudson, 1987.
2. M. Kellmer Pringle, *The Needs of Children*, Hutchinson, 1975.
3. DHSS, *Preparation for Parenthood*, HMSO, 1974; DHSS, *Dimensions of Parenthood*, HMSO, 1974.
4. For a further elaboration of this view of love see M. Scott Peck, *The Road Less Travelled*, Century Hutchinson, 1987.
5. Laurie Lee, *Two Women*, Penguin, 1984.
6. Most of us as parents have the 'hurt child' within our make-up consequent from our own imperfect childhood experiences. This needs to be acknowledged if we are to understand and accept our own shortcomings as parents and act as sustaining spouses in the context of family life. As parents we still have needs to be parented – see, for example A. Jenkins in R.C. Whitfield (ed.) *Families Matter*, Marshall Pickering, 1987.
7. Aspects of support for parents are incorporated in G. Pugh and E. De'Ath, *The Needs of Parents: Practice and Policy in Parent Education*, National Children's Bureau/Mac-

millan, 1984.

8. For an introduction to marriage enrichment see H. and R. Fielder in W. Dryden (ed.), *Marital Therapy in Britain*, Vol. 2, Harper and Row, 1985.

9. See for example Chapter 2 of R.C. Whitfield, Education for Family Life, Hodder and Stoughton, 1980.

10. See for example, R.S. Peters, *Moral Development and Moral Education*, Allen and Unwin, 1981.

11. *Needs of Children*, op. cit., p. 159, reprinted as note 21 below.

12. For a more extensive human and family developmental table (including that in adulthood and involving recapitulation in marriage) see E. Street, Chapter 3, in *Marital Therapy*, op. cit.

13. Dr. James Dobson, an American paediatrician, has over the past decade written some excellent books on child rearing which are, for the most part, available in paperback in the UK. His latest book has the title: *Parenting Isn't for Cowards: Dealing confidently with the frustrations of child rearing*, World Books, 1987.

14. *Families Matter*, op. cit.

15. R.C. Whitfield, Chapter 9 of P. Maher (ed.), *Child Abuse: The Educational Perspective*, Blackwells, 1987.

16. For a case example and policy comment regarding television's role in parent education see R. Whitfield, 'Media in parent education: some signposts from an extended case study prompted by a BBC TV initiative', *Journal of the Institute of Health Education*, Vol. 24, no. 4, 1986, pp. 146–158.

17. *Needs of Children*, op. cit.

18. S. Comber, S. and R. Whitfield, *Liberal Education*, no. 56, 1986, pp. 17–23; D. Harman and O.G. Brim, *Learning to be Parents: Principles, Programs and Methods*, Sage, 1980; see also notes 7, 9, 14 and 15.

19. Adapted from R.C. Whitfield, *Disciplines of the Curriculum*, McGraw Hill, 1971, p. 234.

20. The National Family Trust has recently been established 'to sponsor and execute educational development and related research to promote the strengthening of family life and of marital and family relationships in Britain'. Part of its responsibility is therefore to develop parenthood education initiatives which are not only psychologically informed but also morally based, since the ways in which people treat each other always raise questions of values.

21.   i. Give continuous, consistent, loving care – it's as essential for the mind's health as food is for the body.
  ii Give generously of your time and understanding – playing with and reading to your child matters more than a tidy, smooth-running home.
  iii Provide new experiences and bathe your child in language from birth onwards – they enrich his growing mind.
  iv Encourage him to play in every way both by himself and with other children – exploring, imitating, constructing, pretending and creating.
  v Give more praise for effort than for achievement.
  vi Give him ever-increasing responsibility – like all skills, it needs to be practised.
  vii Remember that every child is unique – so suitable handling for one may not be right for another.
  viii Make the way you show disapproval fit your child's temperament, age and understanding.
  ix Never threaten that you will stop loving him or give him away; you may reject his behaviour but never suggest that you might reject him.
  x Don't expect gratitude; your child did not ask to be born – the choice was yours.

22. *Needs of Children*, op. cit.

8   For the Sake of the Children?

Patricia Morgan

1   Summary and Introduction

The once widely-held belief that parents should do their utmost to preserve their marriage for the sake of the children has been increasingly challenged. Instead it is claimed that the break-up of the home is more beneficial for the children than for them to remain with two parents who do not get on – a claim most widely used among those lobbying for easier divorce. Implicit in this claim is the assumption that a divorce which promotes the happiness of adults inevitably benefits the children as well, thus the parent-child relationship is subsumed into and subjugated by the husband-wife relationship.

Changes in the law also promote the myth that a 'clean break' is always best and incorrectly assume that divorce will bring an end to conflict. Rather, divorce can lead to additional strains caused by the problems of rearing children in a one-parent family. The 'clean break' notion also promotes the idea that it would be best if the non-custodial parent, normally the father, could just drop out of the children's lives and virtually be regarded as *de jure* dead.

These claims are based on early studies which exhibit basic methodological flaws. The first really detailed and adequate study was not published until 1985 but, taken in conjunction with research findings in America, this presents a very different view. Even where divorce was the result of open conflict, children appeared to be more upset following the separation than during the period preceding it. In fact evidence suggests that often divorce does not result from conflict – this only enters the arena after proceedings have been initiated. And from the children's point of view, many regarded their homes as basically 'happy' before the breakup. Only in a few cases, where they have been subject to violence or abuse, do children positively benefit from divorce.

The most common feelings among children of divorced parents are bewilderment, insecurity, rejection and resentment which persist several years after the divorce and are reflected in low levels of educational achievement. Too often, the custodial parent, burdened with the strains of building a new life, alone or with a new partner, has less time for the children's needs and is unaware of their feelings, particularly of continued hopes of reconciliation. Adolescents in particular suffer from lack of control and guidance from parents too involved with their own problems and often become aggressive and precociously preoccupied with sex.

If the detrimental effects of divorce on the children are to be minimised, it is essential that they should maintain a relationship with *both* parents. But this is seldom the case, the majority have lost contact with the non-custodial parent within a relatively short time and all-too often the remaining parent, usually the mother, will extrapolate her own feelings of vindictiveness and self-right eousness onto the children thus souring the relationship with the other parent. Nor can re-marriage substitute for a home with both natural parents, in fact a quarter of children researched, find the acquisition of a step-parent the hardest part of their parents' break-up.

It is time to realise that the interests of adults and children do not necessarily coincide and to restore the idea that parents have a duty to provide their children with an example of self-control and self-denial. This may well mean staying together 'for the sake of the children'.

2   Changing attitudes to divorce: don't stay together just for the sake of the children

Not so long ago, the belief was general that parents who disagreed should suppress or hide their differences in order to preserve the home 'for the sake of the children'. Indeed, around the time of divorce reform in the 1960s, the obvious anxiety of progressives to play down the numbers of children involved in divorce was itself testimony to the dominance of the opinion that broken homes were detrimental to the young. Dependent children, as George Levinger,[1] American authority on divorce, points out, exert a significant barrier force which applies as much to changes in the divorce laws as the decisions of spouses to separate.

However, this soon gave way to the belief that – while problems in children are associated with the breakup of the home following on parental discord, or with unbroken, but conflicted, homes – the breakup of the homes as such is benign. In this, the deficiencies of broken homes are attributed to the defects of marriage themselves, so that the problems really arise from the parents staying together, not splitting up – which they seem to be well advised to do in the interests of the children if tension prevails or trouble looms. Only recently, I overheard two young social workers complaining about 'irresponsible' (and obviously unreconstructed parents) who still insisted on staying together for the sake of the children when they did not get on. What, I wondered, would they have made of the parents of the Victorian writer who, on hearing shouting and swearing coming from their bedroom, asked nanny 'What are they doing?' She told him that they were 'rehearsing a play' and he found that the 'rehearsals went on for twenty years'.

3   Sociologists claim children benefit from easier divorce

The origins of this about turn in attitudes to divorce and children are not difficult to find. In the forefront of the campaign for easier divorce, sociologist O.R. McGregor was asking 'Is it more or less damaging to children to live in a home where, at best, there is no affection between the parents and, at worst, constant open friction; or to face the consequences of a broken home in the care of one parent? He acknowledged 'the complete lack of that scientific and statistical knowledge by which this unhappy dilemma can be resolved' – as the National Association of Mental Health had emphasised before the 1956 (Morton) Commission on divorce. Of course, this did not stop there being religious organisations and schoolteachers pointing to the desirability of keeping children even in actively quarrelsome homes, while on the other side, social workers and probation officers suggested the wisdom of removing children from bad domestic atmospheres. Given this,

O.R. McGregor rapidly concluded that 'The weight of informed opinion' was against those 'institutionalists' who thought that homes should remain intact for 'the sake of the children'. Indeed, he confidently pronounced that:

> As some two-thirds of all divorced persons marry again, the chances that a child of divorced parents may achieve emotional security in a new home are high. The effects of divorce on children are frequently exaggerated.[3]

As such, the position was that 'Children would have nothing to lose, and probably much to gain, from easier and speedier facilities for divorce'.

Obviously, if nothing else, claims that divorce is best for children when parents argue and fight, could be highly serviceable to reformers who would wish to emphasize the advantages of divorce and the perils of a continuing marriage. As M.P.M. Richards and Michael Dyson from the Cambridge Child Care and Development Group observe, it is all too transparent that '...such an argument, if true, would help to achieve a change in the law that some perceive as making divorce "easier"'.[4] It also, of course, legitimises the removal of obstacles to parents' pursuit of their own satisfactions, where they can seek their happiness and gratification without accusations that they are putting the welfare of the young in jeopardy. Indeed, it was not long before one of the ways in which the permissive society was congratulating itself on being the civilised society was with the assertion that modern people were enlightened enough to end their marriages when these were going badly, instead of inflicting 'damaging' conflict on their children. It became 'evidence' for that much reiterated view that '... a relatively high divorce rate may be indicative not of *lower*, but of *higher*, standards of marriage in society'.[5] And, as such, it demonstrated our superiority over our predecessors, so that any increase in divorce or one-parent families has been apt to be represented as some kind of advanced stage of moral development and improvement in child rearing:

> One of the most encouraging changes in family life has been the transition from Victorian emphasis on the duties which children

owed their parents to present stress on the duties of parents to children.[6]

However, no independent criteria have ever been provided for these 'higher standards', apart from the level of the divorce rate where, it seems that the higher this rises, so *ergo*, the higher our standards must be.

4 Satisfaction of parents put before needs of children

Yet, not only is 'conflict' a very elastic concept, but an equation has been made between what is bad for children and what is intolerable or unsatisfactory to adults. Here, the parent-child relationship has been absorbed by the husband-wife relationship, so that the end of the marital partnership has been made to coincide with the termination of the parent-child tie. In turn, a new marriage for the spouse is a 'new family' or a 'new Daddy' for her children. Assumptions are that:

> ...a marriage that is unhappy for the adults is unhappy for the children and, furthermore, that a divorce that promotes the happiness of the adults will inevitably benefit the children as well. This presumed communality of interests and perceptions between adults and children, along with the companion notion that the experience of the children can be subsumed under the experience of the adults, will be called into sharp question by our young subjects.[7]

Of course, it is interesting how the options open to discordant or discontented spouses have been cast in terms of a highly restricted choice of either continuing conflict or divorce. There are, as Martin P.M. Richards and M. Dyson point out:

> ...other possibilities: that the couple resolve their conflicts, or that the marriage might become more characterised by a distant rather than a conflicted relationship. The research shows that distant marriages are much less damaging for children than those with high levels of conflict.[8]

However, these 'other possibilities' receive scant, if any, public recognition because of the persistant dominance of a view of marital breakdown as something in the manner of a naturally determined and inevitable phenomenon. Here, divorce is purely responsive as a sort of regulator of marital behaviour or undertaker for the 'decent burial' of 'dead' or 'hollow-shell' marriages. And, since floundering marriages are construed as fundamentally and irremediably flawed, then it is clearly in the best interests of all concerned to lend their dissolution every assistance – extricating everybody as 'expeditiously and inexpensively' as possible from the war zone, and making sure as you go that the formalities themselves do not throw up roadblocks that give rise to more friction and frustration. This all reached its apotheosis in the parliamentary passage of the Matrimonial and Family Proceedings Bill in 1983/4 (allowing divorce after one year of marriage and formalising 'clean break' arrangements), and the Matrimonial Causes Procedure (Booth) Committee in 1985, which identified the 'major mischief' of divorce proceedings as any of the 'delays and difficulties in achieving finality'.

5   Easier divorce destabilises marriage by promoting idea of terminable contracts

Sadly, the notion that divorce resolves conflict without itself being instrumental in fomenting discord – like the idea that the availability of divorce is irrelevant to the rate at which it is resorted to, has never passed beyond being a comforting and pious expression. It is as conceivable that divorce as much engenders, focuses, accentuates and sustains conflict, or distils it from all manner of disagreements, disharmonies and dissatisfactions, as dampens and dissolves it. In turn, if the feasibility of divorce has any effect on the rate at which it is resorted to, or the degree to which it is considered a viable option by more couples in more circumstances, then it follows that divorce itself is capable of increasing the sum total of both marital breakdown *and* conflict Spouses may feel under less contraint to restrain, resolve or conceal their disagreements, misdemeanours and complaints. That the parties feel able to bale out more easily might arguably put more relationships on a makeshift footing and in a greater state of flux, then if the spouses accepted that some options were more or less foreclosed, or that there were some limits to individual satisfaction.

Inescapably, law will always embody and promote certain moral assumptions, however much anyone may try and maintain that it is value neutral. The new worms about marital behaviour incorporated in the liberal divorce laws lead to marital instability because marriage has become a terminable contract in which minor disputes may readily develop into disruptive conflicts, and which is vulnerable to the predatory activities of interlopers.

6   Divorce may not resolve conflict and can create additional strains

Furthermore, there is no more inherent reason why life *after* divorce should be *conflict free*, than that poor relationships between spouses must negate good relationships *between parents*, or *a parent* and *the children*. In turn, the children of divorce do not just walk off into the sunset. In making any comparison between continuing marriage and divorce, consequences beyond the divorce itself need to be considered. It is just possible that divorce may not remove conflict between the parties and that, in addition, new partners come onto the scene who, in turn, become embroiled in conflict with one or both of the original parents. Second and third marriages, or other liaisons, may be more or less equally subject to conflict as the first, even if the notion is very prevalent that these represent 'happy ever after' sequalae to earlier 'mistakes'. And, even if the parents find happiness elsewhere, this does not necessarily mean that the children are going to take to their new Daddies or Mummies, or even that these new partners will want much to do with the offspring of other unions. As it has turned out, second and third marriages have a far greater chance of breaking down than the first (to the tune of 40 per cent). Similarly, there may be many problems involved in living in a one-parent family which have to be offset against remaining even in a less than ideal intact family. These include, again, the possibility of conflict between the parent and her offspring in a situation which precludes the child having anyone else to turn to.

Certainly, there have been sporadic findings over the years which have purportedly demonstrated the veracity of the conclusion that children in discordant homes are more troubled than

115

those living with one parent. At the same time, numerous studies have documented substantially higher delinquency rates for children whose parents have divorced or separated, with law-breaking hardly raised at all for those who have lost parents by death.[9] However, the far more adverse effects on children of divorce, separation or desertion, compared with death of a parent have been attributed to the comparative lack of conflict in homes affected by bereavement. And, since delinquency is also found in unbroken, but neglectful and quarrelsome homes,[10] this has been used to underline the thesis that it must be the discord preceding the break, rather than the break itself, which leads to the anti-social behaviour, even when the parents eventually split up.

> Delinquency is thus associated with breaks which follow parental discord or discord without a break, but *not* with a break-up of the home as such.

> So, if only – the reasoning has gone – the divorce could be even quicker and 'cleaner' in getting rid of all those 'hollow-shells', we might obviate the conflict and make marital breakdown as benign as widowhood. If only one party could slip out of the child's life and be regarded as *de jure* dead. Indeed, the actual termination of parent-child relationships seems to have emerged as the accepted, even approved, outcome of divorce. In his highly influential text,[12] Michael Rutter passes easily between 'broken home' and 'bond disruption' – where, presumably, the child does not see one of his parents again – and seems to equate or conflate the two.

7 Too ready assumption that father-child relationship expendable

However, this kind of assumption illustrates the abysmal failure of much which passes for psychology to come to terms with the basic propensity of human beings to interpret and explain their experiences. Given this, it cannot really cope with the implications of parental loss where the parent is not involuntarily removed by natural causes, but centres his life elsewhere. It all assumes that children attach little, if any, significance to the departure of a parent or, more precisely, the male parent. (Indeed, there might have been something of an impasse created for the development of 'clean break' divorce if, on the one hand, it was deemed necessary to save children from conflict yet, on the other, they might suffer the loss of either parent equally.) But, assurances have been easily forthcoming from popular psychology that scrutinisation of the 'needs' of children had failed to find any for more than one 'psychological parent'. This has resolved the dilemma by essentially destroying the *raison d'être* of the two-parent home, where the exit of father has become an easily payable price for family harmony.

A result of this has been that legions of fathers have lost their children, and children their fathers, because the courts are loath to insist on access or joint custody against the wishes of the mother in case the child is 'damaged' by the fuss she creates. Overall, there has been as little inclination to question maternal absolutism, as there has been to entertain the possibility that the continuation of the father-child tie may have positive effects which far outweigh any detrimental effects of the mother's anger at her ex-spouse for retaining a place in their children's lives.

8 Faulty methodology and insufficient research used to back up claims that children little affected by divorce

Moreover, there is a basic methodological flaw in those early studies which were used to prove that children in separated families were better off than those in discordant, unbroken homes which essentially made the two groups non-comparable. Thus, while marital discord was rated at the time the children were being assessed, the divorce or separation experienced by the others was often long in the past – so that the timing of the events affecting the children's lives had been disregarded. In fact, considering that, by the time, the effect of divorce on families must already have been considerable, since its sheer size was so immense, it was as late as 1982 that researchers M. Dyson and M.P.M. Richards concluded in a review of the available literature on separation, divorce and children that 'No detailed study of the immediate impact of marital separation on children had been carried out in Britain'.[13] In turn, academics and professionals have been 'very slow to bring what material there is to the attention of the public and those in a position to influence policy'. Changes in family law and the turnover of marriages have continued at a brisk pace both despite this paucity of direct evidence, and a plethora of disturbing findings bearing obliquely on the subject. These suggest that children from one parent families have poorer educational and intellectual attainment; that higher proportions of delinquents come from broken homes and that children in psychiatric clinics have often been through divorce. Moreover, divorced and separated adults make a disproportionate contribution to the amount of serious ill-health, mental disturbance, absenteeism, alcoholism and suicide.

The first detailed study on British children of the effects of divorce was not published until 1985, using a representative Scottish sample.[14] Most evidence had, until then, come from America, where research had started not all that long before. In California, more people were applying for divorce than marriage licences before J.S. Wallerstein and J.B. Kelly began their outstanding study of 60 divorcing families (incorporating 131 children ranging from three to 18 years), which stretched over five years. The sample came from a particularly affluent area with one of the highest divorce rates in America. But, to counter objections about the 'unrepresentive' nature Wallerstein and Kelly

> ...reasoned that precisely because most of these children were not stressed by chronic poverty or the pressures of racism, by overcrowding at home or school, or other similar inner city problems, we would be able to study divorce at its most separable as a vector of change.[15]

It is also helpful in examining the veracity of claims that it is only the unusual or stigmatised status of divorce (or single parents) in Britain that accounts for any observed adverse effects on children – which could be removed if a greater 'diversity' of household arrangements and impermanence of relationships were culturally accepted as 'normal'. The other significant American work on divorce is that of E.M. Hetherington and colleagues, which studied 48 families with a child at nursery school (mean age nearly four at the start of the study) for two years.[16] All the children were in the mother's custody and were studied at home, in school and in the laboratory by observation, various assessment procedures and interviews of all those with any care of them. The significance of this study is that it incorporated a control group of married families, in which a sub-group was identified where conflict was high.

These three imposing studies with their very different methods and project designs, now provide a fairly comprehensive analysis of children's experiences of divorce and its effects on their development. The unanimity of the findings from both sides of the Atlantic is astonishing, particularly considering the disparate samples.

9   Domestic conflict can harm children but isn't necessarily resolved by divorce

Certainly domestic discord, or varieties of this, is associated with problems in children.[17] But, perhaps not surprisingly,[18] there are big differences in children's adjustment between families with and without open conflict, or conflict that embroiled and distressed the children. The Hetherington team[19] compared separated children with those in intact families rated as having either intense or low levels of conflict. Near the time of separation and for a year of follow up children were more upset than those in conflict ridden marriages. But, by two years their problems had fallen below those in marriages with continuing high conflict. However these children were very young and other evidence (see below) indicates how older children are far more adversely affected by parental separation. Moreover, if the overall problems of children increase as the period of conflict continues in intact marriages, so too an improvement in the situation leads to an improvement in the children – without the intervention of a divorce.

At the same time, many divorces appear to have little or nothing to do with marital incompatibility, let alone open conflict. Thus, Judith B. Wallerstein and Joan B. Kelly could only characterise one third of divorces they studied as undertaken rationally to undo an unhappy marriage which was unlikely to change. Other divorces followed, for example, on a stressful experience which had nothing to do with the marriage, like an unexpected death, an accident, or the sudden onset of psychiatric illness:

Mrs K filed for divorce shortly after her mother died. Her husband, a gentle, devoted family man, was startled and begged her to change her mind, or at least permit him to stay in the family house, since he had no place to go. The children cried and implored their mother to change her mind...Four years later, Mrs K told us "I wish I could marry him again. I was upset. My mother had died, and I felt that he was not sympathetic...It was a terrible mistake, but there is nothing to do now. I have ruined the lives of four people".[19]

Further, divorces are impulsive and resorted to out of anger, jealousy or to get the other spouse's attention; so that proceedings may be started in order to punish the other spouse, or restore the marital tie after an affair. In addition divorce may be encouraged by doctors, therapists or social workers, who identify needs for self realisation in their clients and get them to share the conviction that marriage is a hindrance to their freedom and development. While the fullest accounts of the motivation for divorce are in American material, there are reasons to believe that the situation is similar here. There is widespread evidence that those who consult solicitors over marital difficulties are quickly precipitated into legal proceedings. In turn, the basis upon which the law has developed since the first big reform is that discontented, aggrieved or disorientated spouses must be promptly steered towards one gate, discouraged from having second thoughts and propelled through the process as quickly as possible. Considering this, it is perhaps not all that surprising that survey material from Britain indicates that, like America, as many as 50 per cent of men and at least 25 per cent of women feel later that divorce was the wrong decision and wish that they were still married.

However, once the divorce process is under way, then it is calculated to produce or exacerbate conflict even where this hardly, or never existed before. Relationships between the spouses are likely to deteriorate spectacularly and it is often at this point that 'irretrievable breakdown' essentially occurs. Disagreements are now no longer likely to be concealed, restrained or resolved, and all the truces, cross border alliances and fraternisation that may be present even in relatively tense, or discordant homes, are likely to be rapidly abandoned as the spouses join battle to get the biggest share of the spoils. In divorce, all

>...the mutual ties that served sometimes to restrain the expression of hostility during the marriage are broken. Agitated... the partners to divorce often finish off whatever last vestiges of good feeling might have remained in the marriage.[21]

10 Few children aware of unhappiness before parental break-up

As Ann Mitchell found in Britain, very few children are relieved that their parents separate. Asked about their family life before separation, about three-quarters recalled that this had been happy. Only one in five said that the marriage had been their most difficult times. While half the children did not remember any parental conflict before separation, those who did describe argument still did not think this sufficient reason for parental separation. Many were surprised when their parents separated: 'I know my parents argued and had tried not to in front of me, but I'd not expected them to split'.[22] Given all this, and the fact that two-thirds of parents had not provided any explanation at all

>Many children had been bewildered, not knowing whether the separation was to be short or permanant and not believing parental arguments to be sufficient reason for breaking up the family. If the reason had been obvious to the parents, the children did not necessarily agree.[23]

These results are similar to those of J.T. Landis in 1960, who had been surprised to find that 82 per cent of American college students whose parents were divorced, later rated themselves as happy or very happy before the break-up.[24] And, as in Ann Mitchell's study, they did not necessarily equate conflict with an unhappy family life. Many of them would have preferred to remain with an unbroken family, where there was at least the hope that parents would stop arguing. And again, the same story is found in a recent British investigation involving 100 children (which, while it was unrepresentative in obtaining its respondents through advertisement, broke new ground just before Ann Mitchell). Here, Y. Walczck and S. Burns found that children experienced their parents' separation

with disbelief and longed for reconciliation.[25] Many did not consider parental disagreements to be grounds for ending the marriage
and only a quarter were relieved when their parents separated.

11 Divorce creates feelings of insecurity, rejection and resentment leading to low attainment

The children caught up in all of this tend to feel angry, unhappy,
rejected and embarrassed. Their need to make sense of what is
happening to them is centred both on dealing with all the conflict
and, often much more, *comprehending the disappearance of one
parent*. Overwhelmingly, children's misery centres upon the departure of the father. Children under five have a tendency to blame
themselves for his loss and to be anxious that if one parent has
gone, then so might the other, or they are frightened of being sent
away. Findings are that many children in this age range, who tend
to be aggressive, irritable and fearful, are actually worse a year
later, even where open conflict was not present in the divorces.
Slightly older children express wishes and entertain fantasies about
reconciliation where, J.S. Wallerstein and J.B. Kelly found hardly
any pleased or relieved about the divorce, even if widespread and
severe conflict existed in their families. Even a year later a third of
eight year olds still wanted reconciliation.

However, a phenomenon which grows with age is anger and hostility towards the parent or parents who the child or adolescent
believes inititated a separation for which they can usually see no
justification. Boys particularly blame their mothers for causing the
break, or driving their father away. Fears and anxieties are still
common, with about a quarter of children over nine reported as
worrying about being abandoned or forgotten. Understandably,
they tend to feel lonely and peripheral to the family as the parents
become preoccupied with their own concerns. The deterioration
which J.S. Wallerstein and J.B. Kelly found for both behaviour and
school performance in a half of older children has, of course, been
frequently observed where those affected by divorce have been
compared to children from intact families. Research from the
Hetherington team is in line – not only with the frequent reports of
teachers on the disruptive effect of divorce on school work – but all

the studies of one-parent families which have repeatedly shown how aggressive behaviour, insecurity and lack of control at home and school are heightened after marital separation, particularly in boys. And, while this might show some decrease two years later, it is still marked – as is the deterioration in intellectual functioning. Reports of reduced school performance or achievement and lower IQs are common for one-parent (particularly mother-headed) 'families'.[26] For example, the large-scale, longitudinal National Child Development Study of children from birth to adulthood has showed significant differences for social adjustment and school attainment between children in intact and one parent 'families', at every age the sample has been investigated.[27] These are most marked for children from divorced and separated families – whenever the breakup actually occurred.

12   Divorce undermines attitudes to morality, especially among adolescents

Something which is apparent for older children from broken homes which becomes more marked with adolescents is a precocious pre-occupation with both assertiveness and sex. This is probably owed in part to the fact that teenagers in separating families often lack controls and guidance from parents who are too involved with themselves and their problems to provide a secure home base. The adolescent needs a resilient and dependable family from which he can venture out and use as a yardstick for comparing and assessing other relationships. The stress and dissolution which the family undergoes at separation means that he is denied this supportive and stable background, as the adults in his life become as confused and vulnerable as he is. Parents may, indeed, reverse roles and call upon older children to protect and support them in becoming 'parents to their own parents'.

But, what also needs to be borne in mind is the fact that while parental sexuality is relatively opaque or invisible in the intact family, it often becomes obvious at separation, both through quarrels and accusations and the introduction of new partners into the home. Adolescents are preoccupied with sexuality anyway and may be particularly sensitive to cues and models provided by parents, particularly when some mothers begin to dress and behave like young girls and more or less compete with their own daughters for men. Some children begin their own sexual relationships after the discovery of their parents' extra-marital relationships. Moreover, since it is adolescents who are most profoundly grieved by parental separation; most likely to see it in a negative way, and most prone to accuse the parents, this has to be ut in the context of adolescence as a time for the clarification of moral rules. Here, anger at the parents because of the divorce merges into moral indignation and outrage that the parent who has been correcting their conduct is behaving in an immoral and irresponsible fashion. As children's consciences are undermined by the disenchantment with those who acted as moral authorities, so they too feel at liberty to indulge their impulses with impunity. Thus, the very common aggressiveness of children

> ...was doubtless stimulated by witnessing parental fighting and the children's not illogical conclusion that direct expression of intense anger had become acceptable. Beyond this, the children considered the divorce an act of selfishness in which the parents had given primary consideration to their own needs and only secondary consideration to the children. Some youngsters bitterly resented the destruction of their family and their home and they felt betrayed by what they considered the unbecoming, immoral behaviour of a parent...[28]

With divorce, there tends to come pressure on the adolescent to forego the usual help and guidance and achieve independence as quickly as possible. With the mother courting or marrying again, the home may be effectively disbanded. A proportion of adolescents increase in maturity and responsibility (where they may help to keep the household running), but an equal number find early independence in cutting loose from the family and all its problems. The consequent involvement of adolescents in sexual activities and gangs or peer groups is a general reaction to insubstantial domestic relationships and sparse home lives among children from single parent families. In turn, there is a common belief that teenage pregnancies and illegitimate births are more frequent for girls whose parents have separated. The available data suggests that these assumptions are far from prejudice.

13   Only minority of children benefit from divorce – largely by chance

The 10 to 20 per cent of children who actually feel relieved that their parents have separated are – like the ones who make the positive gains after divorce – those who have got away from an abusive or otherwise destructive parent. Where parents were violent, insane, neglectful and rejecting then, indeed, divorce may be in a child's 'best interests' – so long as the post-divorce environment *is* an improvement on the previous one, for it need not be. Otherwise, very few children identify with the parents' wish to escape from a marriage, even if they know that this is unhappy. And, again, it is only when the child voluntarily places a step-parent in the parental role that *substitution* occurs as the active choice of a child who has usually been maltreated or repudiated by his original parent.

But, it is in few, if any, divorces that a parent's destructive, abusive behaviour towards the children is among the acknowledged events leading to separation – even where women may be tyrannised by the same violent or disturbed men who ill-treat, or neglect the children. Indeed, there may very well be collusion between spouses in the maltreatment of children – whether they separate or not. Thus, if a spouse divorces a destructive partner and the children benefit – this is largely coincidental.

14   Stress caused by divorce can lead to neglect of children's needs

If this is the position with separations where parents' relationship to the children is effectively non-existent, antagonistic or damaging, then it should hardly be surprising that other parents in far less adverse circumstances do not divorce their partner because they have made some sensitive appraisal of the needs of their children. Instead, they are more likely to be in too much of a turmoil themselves to 'appreciate what they are doing to their children'.[29] As Ann Mitchell found, divorcing parents are so caught up in their own sadness and anger that their children often cannot turn to them for emotional support 'My Mum didn't understand how I felt. She was too busy being angry'.[30] Indeed, they might later admit that they had not considered the effects of separation on their children. As one mother commented:

> "I can see now they'd have been better off with both parents. I was thinking of myself when I asked my husband to leave. At the time of going through it, you never think of that. You're not thinking of the future, you're going from day to day. You are more concerned with your own life." One father was surprised, in the interview, to realize that he had never, at any time, given any thought to his children's feelings.[31]

At the point where a child needs extra help from his parents, the parents are at the centre of conflict and too preoccupied with themselves to even notice their children's feelings. Unlike stress originating outside the family, the stress of divorce, and the child's difficulty in coping with it, is compounded by the involvement of one or both parents as its central source. The child's life is disrupted by a parent – the same parent whose 'inner turmoil renders him or her insensitive to the child's needs...'[32] Underlining the observations of Wallerstein and Kelly and Ann Mitchell, Hetherington's analysis of parent-child relations also showed parents to be less affectionate, less controlling, less able to communicate with their children and more inconsistent – with distress peaking about a year after the divorce in this study.[33] A plethora of material now shows how much separated spouses suffer from depression, nervous disorders or sheer exhaustion, which makes them unfit, or unable, to function properly as parents. Robert Chester's[34] analysis of the reports made by a sample of women petitioners for divorce about their health showed that a majority experienced a deterioration with an emphasis on symptoms related to stress.

15 Detrimental effects of divorce by no means confined to immediate aftermath

Of course, it might be maintained that all these troubles are temporary and that along the lines of the 'conflict avoidance' thesis, the long term benefits of separation – for adults and child alike – are well worth the initial upheavals. However, it appears that the ability of adults to function as parents is often severely reduced not only by the turmoil of the divorce period – but also afterwards in that they are coping alone, establishing further relationships or continuing the feuds with their ex-spouse.

If J.S. Wallerstein and J.B. Kelly reported little connection between the extent of the initial reaction of young children to marital separation and the course of recovery, then this was because improvement was related to the quality of parental care and the degree to which strife between parent and child, or the parents themselves, continued. Thus, mothers who continued to be obsessed with their own hurt and anger were unable to help children who found them 'powerful and terrifying in their potential for destruction'. Children are especially burdened when divorce makes no sense, brings no relief to any identified family conflict and the pain of the family disruption adds to the pain of the initial unhappiness. Unfortunately, parents are commonly found bad-mouthing each other and demanding that their children support them in hostilities long after a divorce. The gory details of the marriage are preserved, polished up and endlessly reiterated. Who has not heard the lone parent who stridently holds forth, in front of the children, on how she pulled up the home by its bootstraps when 'he left and now 'doesn't care a damn about any of us'?

Even after 18 months separation, many issues are unresolved in the lives of parents and children. Feelings of anger, rejection and humiliation are still intense and most adults have still not established stability and continuity in their lives. In California, J.S. Wallerstein and J.B. Kelly found that, even after five years, children were well aware that their parents were still bitter towards each other. Unfortunately, all observation suggests how continuing conflict after the divorce is associated with high levels of problems in the children. Indeed, *conflict in divorced families*, in all its varieties (whether between ex-spouses, the parent and child, or with third parties), *is more damaging than high levels of conflict in married families*, especially for boys. This may be explained in terms of the absence of a protective parental buffering, which the second parent provides in two-parent families. This goes some way to compensate for the disorientating effects of domestic conflict or poor

127

relations between the child and one parent. In turn, Richards and Dyson[35] feel that this may account for the findings of other studies,[36] that a positive relationship with one parent in intact families appears to reduce the impact of an adverse relationship with the other parent. In two-parent families, parents compensate for each others deficiencies and supplement each other, so that where there is marital discord, children who have a good relationship with one parent are less likely to develop behaviour problems than where there are poor relations with both parents.

16 Links with non-custodial parent important but seldom maintained

Exactly parallel to this is the way in which it has been found that a good paternal relationship for children in broken homes was beneficial in proportion as the contact with the father was maintained.[37] But, unfortunately, a positive relationship with one parent which might help to mitigate the deleterious effects of either inter-parent conflict or a poor relationship between mother and child is 'less likely to happen in a single parent family where the child sees his non-custodial parent intermittently or not at all'.[38] This lack becomes more apparent over time and it may be surmised that this reflects the gradual withdrawal of contact with the father. Vindictive and self-righteous – like the mothers in Ann Mitchell's study – custodial parents may not only do nothing to hide their feelings from the children, but are often glad to find all manner of reasons to reduce or stop the father's visits. In America, J.A. Fulton[39] found that a half of the parents in his study had on occasions refused access to their ex-spouses in order to punish them. If visits do take place, they may provide opportunities to air grievances and collect ammunition. The child may be bribed with gifts and treats and 'becomes the instrument for each parent to prove that the other parent's care is inadequate and the cause of the child's unhappiness'. Nearly half of the divorced mothers interviewed by W.J. Goode[40] in 1965 wanted their children to have less access to fathers or none at all. Times have not changed, with Ann Michell finding that one fifth of the parents in her survey definitely did not want their children having any access to the other parent (most of these had successfully discouraged any continuing contact). Indeed, only a quarter of her custodial parents expressed any positive attitude towards their children keeping in touch with the other parent.[41] Not surprisingly, given these attitudes, it appears that around 25 per cent of children have lost contact with their fathers within a couple of months of their parents separating and that this rises to around a half by the time that the divorce proceedings are concluded.[42]

17 Parents too ready to extrapolate their own feelings to their children and often totally unaware of children's true feelings

But, as much after as during divorce, parents overwhelmingly and unreflectively ascribe their own feelings to their children. They are as much unaware of their children's wishes for continued contact with both parents as they are for information and understanding. They tell themselves that a 'clean break' is far better for the children when mother and father are not getting on and, if they are glad to be divorced, then they also believe that their children's lives must have been improved because their own has. Even mothers who worried about the effects of separation on their children still think that their lives must, after all, have changed for the better:

> …possibly feeling some guilt for having moved straight to a new partner [parents] played down their children's feelings. "She was temporarily upset, but it was nothing to keep her unhappy, and she could see it was for the best". Only 10 of the 72 parents thought that their children had cried at all. "Christine used to cry and say that no one wanted her". Most said this had not lasted for long: "both boys cried their eyes out, but they got over it after four months", said the father who thought his sons had put their distress behind them.[43]

Yet, the Californian study, for example, showed that over a third of children were intensely unhappy and dissatisfied with their lives *five years after the separation* (with 56 per cent still finding no improvement over the pre-divorce family). Indeed, although the number of unhappy children was highest at the time of parental separation, this had declined at 18 months to rise again by the five year follow-up mark. Both boys and girls lived for years with feelings of rejection, particularly from the same sex parent, where it was especially boys – who all lived with their mothers – and were aged six to 12 at the time of separation, who felt most rejected and wondered how their fathers could have left. (Overall, 39 per cent felt rejected by fathers and 17 per cent by mothers.) Less than a quarter were now relieved that their parents had parted, although 34 per cent appeared to be doing well and coped successfully at home and school. However, 37 per cent of the sample were moderately or severely depressed and there was a fair amount of anti-social behaviour. Similarly, in Britain, Ann Mitchell found that whereas two-thirds of the children had been upset by the separation, less than a third of the parents thought that they had been adversely affected in any way so that, all in all, when children claimed that mothers still did not understand their distress, they were right:

> Alison was profoundly deaf and was interviewed with her mother as interpreter. She showed her feelings about the separation by indicating tears running down her cheeks, to her mother's astonishment and indignation.[44]

One child in six in Ann Mitchell's sample admitted to still wishing that their parents would be reunited many years later – often even after one or both had remarried. Twice as many had entertained hopes for a few years that their parents would be reconciled. In total, over half had wanted reconciliation, whether they imagined it possible or not.

18   Divorce puts greater pressure on remaining parent at a time when least able to cope

In the absence of one parent, the quality of the remaining one becomes far more important. If, after separation, fathers have a declining influence on the child's self-control and other development, so the child's relationship with the mother becomes more closely related to his behaviour. Understandably, the kind of structure provided by more authoritative mothers gives children the direction and control that is so necessary under the conditions of stress and change so often associated with divorce. Yet, mothers are most likely to be disorientated and disorganised in the conditions of family breakup and the situation need not improve with time. As Richards and Dyson observe, the '...change from marriage to single living for both men and women involves a major upheaval in almost all spheres of life'.[45] And here, the parent-child relationship may deteriorate against a background of chaotic living, with erratic meals and bedtimes, where a vicious circle is set up by

> ... an unhappy combination of children who are likely to be aggressive, disobedient and so on, faced with parents who are less than usually able to cope. Each no doubt feeds the stress and pain of the other. This pattern of disorganisation seems particularly characteristic of mothers and sons.[46]

In this, the two major American studies report the same decline in the quality of many mother-child relations as they became single parent families – whence they were more conflict ridden, less gratifying and more limited.

Obviously, in one parent families, the lone adult has to perform the child rearing tasks usually shared between two in other homes. As the ratio of children to adults rises, parental attention is more thinly spread, and this is a factor in explaining the poorer performance of children from larger families (in all socio-economic classes), as well as those from one parent families. Moreover, it is not only that two parents can also supplement each other and compensate or help to make up for the other's deficiencies but in any enterprise, including child rearing, standards are maintained, performance improved and excesses checked by the expectations and responses of other people. Those on their own do not receive the kind of feedback for their efforts which tell them that what they are doing is right and worthwhile. If, without the confirmation and collaboration of others, confidence and sense of purpose easily decline, then this reminds us only too well that human beings were designed to be part of groups. In fact, the mother-child tie appears to be difficult to sustain in the absence of another supportive adult, so that it is likely to deteriorate into mutual antagonism. All told, the one parent 'family' is tremendously fragile and extraordinarily susceptible to conflicting stresses from within and depreciations from without.[47] Given this, divorce need not improve the parent's life, let alone the children's. As J.S. Wallerstein and J.B. Kelly found, lifelong states of disorganisation and dissatisfaction were likely to be exacerbated by divorce, where 31 per cent of the men and 42 per cent of the women in their study had not achieved social or psychological stability even five years later. (With a third and a fifth respectively claiming that they were troubled and unhappy).

19 Children often relegated to back seat after divorce

For all manner of reasons, from expanded work schedules to depression, the remaining parent may be substantially less available to the children after a divorce. But, prominent among these is the way in which many parents embark on a flurry of social and sexual activity (where it is precisely part of the ethos of divorce that it is a 'gateway' to a new life and new relationships). The result is that children are more likely to go home to empty houses, put themselves to bed, to be rarely taken out and get their own meals. Older children, particularly, are inclined to feel that parental attention has been entirely withdrawn. Not only may new interests and relationships absorb a major part of the custodial parent's energies and leisure time, but these relationships may break up – with all the resultant turmoil and stress. The children are exposed to more conflict as they attempt to cope with and even comfort a parent depressed or distraught at their lovers' departures. The making and breaking of relationships with boyfriends, or the comings and goings of cohabitees are all bound to multiply the occasions for emotional crises and domestic disputes.

20 Re-marriage often more damaging to children than divorce

Given that it is the disruption or even severance of the relationship with one parent, usually the father, which is implicated in much of the adverse impact of divorce on children, then what evidence there is suggests that this process is much accelerated by the remarriage of either parent. Therefore, it is not surprising that one in four of the children in Ann Mitchell's study found the acquisition of a step-parent the hardest part of their parents' breakup.

Experience suggests that the individual children who benefit from stepfamilies are those who have been parted from psychiatrically ill or abusive parents. This all depends upon their custodial parent rejecting their former spouses treatment and view of themselves and the child being able to turn to an accepting step-parent. Otherwise, one parent homes with an absent father, and those where the mother has remarried appear to be similar in the way in which children from both stepfather and lone mother households are poorer school attenders, have poorer health and behave more badly compared to children from either unbroken homes or step-mother families. Reflecting the malign results of disrupting the relationship with the original parent of the same sex, the National Child Development Study found that 19 per cent of boys in step-father families ended up in court compared with only eight per cent of those still with both original parents (and 20 per cent of boys from stepfamilies had dealings with the police or probation services compared to only nine per cent from unbroken homes). Boys with step mothers had less involvement with the police than those from mother only homes.

This rather gloomy picture of remarriage must be set in the context of the far greater chance of second and third marriages failing, where indications are that conflict in these is more detrimental than conflict in first marriages. Also, it must be remembered that more children are likely to be living in homes where the custodial parent (usually the mother), is cohabiting on either a regular or intermittent basis with one or a succession of men. There is no research on the effects upon children of living with (what must often be) transient and casual relationships. From what we already know, there is no reason to expect that the results would be encouraging.

There is increasing resentment against new partners by children as they get older and step-parents are, in turn, less inclined to be interested, or put any effort into, creating a home for children from a previous union. As the interests of parents and children increasingly diverge, those of the young are not infrequently likely to be peripheral, if not antithetical, to the relationship between the parent and her new partner.

21 'Ideal' divorce – that which achieves greatest continuity with preceding marriage

In stepfamilies, children adjust best on the same basis that they do well in any home – that is, where they not only build a relationship (in this case) with the step-parent but maintain their ties with the original parent and live in a home that is not marked by open conflict. The paradox of the stepfamily is that the child is likely to have less difficulties adjusting to the new partner if he has a good relationship with the non-resident parent. *Personal significance and identity are profoundly related to and affected by the child's sense of connection to his family of origin.* The possible adverse effects of stepfamilies are most likely to be averted or mollified by these relinquishing the very notion that so often seems to make them so attractive in the first place – that they can, or should, replace the original family as a 'fresh start' and a 'complete break' with the past. For most children there are really no such things as second or 'reconstituted' families *since their own parents are irreplaceable.*

Likewise, the post-divorce situation is only benign to the degree that parent-child relationships can be maintained at the level which existed in the pre-divorce family or, if there were difficulties, these can be improved upon. Families where children show a reasonable outcome five or more years later are ones which have been able to re-stablilise or restore their parenting after an initial (and often protracted) disorganised transition period. In this, the factors which mitigate the effects of family breakdown on children involve the extent to which the parents can put aside their own anger and conflicts and retain their joint commitment to the children. Part of this means that the children maintain stable, close relationships with both parents, where they have contact with the non-resident parent on a regular and sufficient enough basis to share everyday life. In turn, the resident parent must allow access without tension and contrive to be positive about her ex-husband to the children. Indeed, the capacity of divorced mothers to function effectively is critically related to the behaviour of the divorced father and the relationship between the ex-spouses.

As such, this 'ideal divorce' has to preserve the cake it eats and recreate something like the child rearing conditions of the harmonious, intact home. All of it demands a measure of self-control, detachment, magnanimity and farsightedness on the part of the divorcees when, with the great majority of people in these inauspicious circumstances, these virtues may not be very well developed and, in many cases, be scarcely present at all. It is highly difficult to sustain previous relationships as if divorce had never been, when the whole point of the exercise is to dis-establish one union so that the parties are free for alternative arrangements, particularly where our notion of divorce has been so sharply drawn in terms of the 'clean break'. It should be clear that marriage is designed to facilitate what divorce is made to thwart – the child's continuous access to two adults for whom his welfare is their joint and paramount concern. This is all best ensured by parents staying put where their children are part of, rather than a burden upon, their current aspirations and concerns.

22   No 'clean break' from children's point of view

To the children, the parents' marriage is essentially indissoluble. For them, divorce cannot be a 'clean break' and the pursuit of that 'finality' (emphasized in the recent Booth Report, 1985) is antithetical to their interests. Any consideration of children means that parents are going to be involved with each other for a long time after the break. If this is inconvenient, frightening and uncomfortable for adults, then they may have to find other ways of managing their feelings than through a 'clean break'.[48]

Unfortunately, there is no blinking the conclusion that divorce is clearly an independent, and increasing, source of problems afflicting the school population. A substantial and growing minority of children involved in divorce at any one time means that there is a correspondingly substantial and growing addition to the numbers of disorientated disturbed and disruptive children. Even if development effects are temporary (an optimistic interpretation), the road to stability is, as researchers now emphasize, far longer than people realise. Moreover, 'what may appear to be a reasonable expectation within the time sense of an adult has a different dimension and meaning in the life of a child'.[49] Two or three years of instability represent a significant part of a child's entire life. The child's unhappy awareness of the parents' distress may extend over many years in the newly divorced family and the sadness and loss is lifelong. As Ann Mitchell observed, her work leaves an '...abiding impression...of young people who have lost some of their childhood and have grown up sad and bewildered' where 'for every woman who claims that divorce has improved her life, there are two children who are inconsolable.' [50]

23   More needs to be done to maintain ties between children and *both* parents following divorce

Of course, children could be given greater consideration in the divorce process if the courts put a 'stronger emphasis on the continuing role of both parents, pointing more clearly to the division between the change in the parents' relationship with each other and...that of each parent and child'.[51] Parents should not be able to divorce themselves or each other from the children and, in this a court-based system of hearings and conciliation; a presumption (or insistence) on joint custody and a greater emphasis on access might help. But, while these or other changes might mollify some of the worst aspects of marital breakdown they do not constitute that much sought panacea that is going to 'take the sting out of divorce'. They may be an advance on the present state of affairs and the best which can be done in a bad situation, but the beneficial effect is likely to be limited.

Even where the post-divorce involvement of non-residential parents is particularly high, there is still a steady decline in contact as time goes by.[52] In speaking of what better to do after divorce we are not discussing the best ways to bring up children. Instead, what we are doing is choosing between less than ideal situations or the lesser of evils. To demand that divorce hurt nobody is to ask the impossible where, as the authors of *The Future of Marriage* observed, the 'best way to reduce pain on divorce is to preserve stable marriages'.[54]

24 Claims that divorce 'best for children' soothe parental consciences

Here, the first step is to stop fooling ourselves that divorce is always the best alternative for the children, or that it could be so contrived to spare them suffering and even do them good. Despite the fictions put out by the media and the 'helping' professions, the nature of parent-child relationships are such that divorce is not, and can never be, in the 'interests of children', unless the parent-child tie is itself absent, or abrogated by rejection, abuse or neglect. In all this, it is no use turning to blame 'Society's ambivalence towards the breaking and remaking of families'[55] for the dilemma, when that 'society' partly consists of children who want their own parents, not new ones or 'reconstituted' families – thrust upon them by processes not of their own choosing.

Unfortunately, the 'needs' attributed to children have been to a large extent projections of their elders' feelings and interests. Much of the reasoning about children being 'better off' away from a 'miserable' home life has been little better than self-serving bunkum to assuage the consciences of parents, reformers and professionals. In reality, divorce is not about ensuring that children get better parents, but the parents' right to happiness and self-fulfilment. A truly remarkable amount of high-minded self-deception has gone into pretending that it is otherwise. Given this, it is not surprising that we should find parents divorcing when they get on well with the children, and couples who stick together despite the fact that one or both may ill-treat their offspring. In turn, when claims are made that high rates of making and breaking marriages are indicative of higher standards or aspirations, we must ask higher standards for whom? The parents' satisfaction and the level of care and concern for the children are not identical, so that the parental pursuit of gratification may easily mean that children receive less, rather than the same or more, consideration.

25 Parents should be made more aware of duty they have to their children

For their part, children usually '…prefer to keep their parents together, even if they do not get on with each other'. That the interests of adults and children may not necessarily coincide was perhaps appreciated by those parents who, while they may not ever have got on well with each other, at least co-operated to maintain the home. Where there is conflict, the best arrangement – after all – may very well be the one where parents stay together and manage to present a united, tranquil and 'normal' front. Unfortunately, the present poor visibility and status of this option means that the technique, as much as the model, is not readily available to troubled couples. Yet, in the past it was by no means uncommon for children to grow up happily and ignorant that their parents had more or less come to an agreement to lead separate lives where this did not impinge upon their duties to the young – including that of setting a good example.:

> The impression given overall by the men in this study, who answered fully with regard to their mothers and fathers, was that obvious discord between parents was unusual. One man said, with some humour, that it did not occur to him that his mother and father did not get on with each other until he was about 25 years old. The impression given by these men is that their mothers maintained respect for the status and role of their fathers, even if an intimate relationship did not exist between them.[56]

This, like the conduct and toleration of an adulterous affair (so long as it did not threaten the continuity of the home), recognised that parenting was an investment which demanded protection and a great deal of self-control and self-denial. It also acknowledged that the home was an educational environment, where the adults' behaviour provided lessons for children in inter-personal conduct. The parents themselves may not have always been able to keep to the ideals they aspired to, but at least they endeavoured to demonstrate to the young how things *should be*.

Notes and References

1. George Levinger, 'Marital cohesiveness and disillusion: integrative review' *Journal of Marriage and the Family* 27, 1965, pp. 19–28; George Levinger and Oliver Moles

(eds.), *Divorce and Separation*, Basic Books, 1975.
2. O.R. McGregor, *Divorce in England*, Wm. Heineman, 1957.
3. Ibid., pp. 167–168.
4. M.P. Richards and Michael Dyson, *Separation, Divorce and the Development of Children*, Cambridge Child Care and Development Group, 1982.
5. Ronald Fletcher, *Britain in the Sixties: the Family and Marriage*, Penguin, revised edition 1966, p. 213.
6. *Divorce in England*, op. cit., p. 102.
7. Judith S. Wallerstein and Joan Berlin Kelly, *Surviving the Breakup: How Children and Parents Cope with Divorce*, Grant McIntyre, 1968.
8. *Separation...*, op. cit., p. 77.
9. F.I. Nye, 'Child Adjustments in Broken and in Unhappy Unbroken Homes', *Marriage and Family Living*, 19, 1957, pp. 356–361.
10. S. Glueck and E.T. Glueck, *Unravelling Juvenile Delinquency*, Commonwealth Fund, N.Y., 1950.
11. W. McCord and J. McCord, *The Origins of Crime: A New Evaluation of the Cambridge-Somervill Youth Study*, University Press, 1959.
12. Michael Rutter, *Maternal Deprivation Reassessed*, Penguin, 1972, p. 108.
13. *Separation...*, op. cit., p. 16.
14. Ann Mitchell, *Children in the Middle*, 1985.
15. *Surviving the Breakup*, op. cit., p. 8.
16. E.M. Hetherington, M. Cox and R. Cox, 'The Aftermath of Divorce', in J.H. Stevens and M. Matthews (eds.), *Mother-Child, Father-Child Relations*, NAEYC, 1977; also 'Family interaction and the social, emotional and cognitive development of children following divorce' in V. Vaughan and T. Brazleton, *The Family: Setting Priorities*, Science and Medicine, 1979.
17. *Maternal Deprivation*, op. cit.,
18. C. Longfellow, 'Divorce in context: its impact on children', in *Divorce and Separation*, op. cit.
19. 'Family interaction', op. cit.
20. *Surviving the Breakup*, op. cit., p. 20.
21. Ibid., p. 26.
22. *Children in the Middle*, op. cit., p. 103.
24. J.T. Landis, 'The trauma of children when parents divorce', *Marriage and Family Living*, 22, 1960, pp. 7–13.
25. Y. Walczck and S. Burns, *Divorce: the child's point of view*, Harper & Row, 1984.
26. H.B. Hiller, *Paternal Deprivation: Family, Schools, Sexuality and Society*, Heath Lexington Books; 1974.
27. Ken Fogelman (ed.) *Growing up in Britain: Papers from the National Child Development Study*, Macmillan for the National Children's Bureau, 1983; E. Ferri, *Growing Up in a One-Parent Family: A Long-term Study of Child Development*, NFER, 1983.
28. *Surviving the Breakup*, op. cit., p. 50.
29. *Children in the Middle*, op. cit., p. 151.
30. Ibid., p. vii.
31. Ibid., p. 88.
32. *Surviving the Breakup*, op. cit., p. 36.
33. 'Aftermath of Divorce', op. cit.
34. Robert Chester, 'Health and Marriage Problems', *Journal of the British Society of Preventive Medicine*, 25, 1971, pp., 231–235.
35. *Separation...*, op. cit.
36. *Maternal Deprivation*, op. cit.
37. *Surviving the Breakup*, op. cit.
38. *Separation...*, op. cit., p. 19.
39. J.A. Fulton, 'Parental Reports of Children's Post Divorce Adjustment', *Journal of*

Social Issues, Vol. 35, No. 4, 1979, pp. 126–139.

40. *Children and Divorce*, Church of England Children's Society, 1983; W.J. Goode, *Women In Divorce*, Free Press, 1965.

41. *Children in the Middle*, op. cit.; P. Wheeler, *Divided Children*, Gingerbread and Families Need Fathers, 1982.

42. Ann Mitchell, *Someone to Turn to: Experiences of Help before Divorce*, Aberdeen University Press, 1981.

43. *Children in the Middle*, op. cit., p. 86; D. Marsden, *Mothers Alone*, 1969.

44. *Children in the Middle*, op. cit., p. 100.

45. *Separation...*, op. cit., p. 20.

46. Ibid., p. 21.

47. *Surviving the Breakup*, op. cit.

48. *Separation...*, op. cit.

49. *Surviving the Breakup*, op. cit.

50. *Children in the Middle*, op. cit.

51. *Separation...*, op. cit., p. 77.

52. 'Aftermath of Divorce', op. cit.

53. *Separation...*, op. cit.

54. *The Future of Marriage*, Society of Conservative Lawyers, 1981, p. 27.

55. Jeanette Kupfermann in *The Times*, 28 November, 1984.

56. Judy Blendis, 'Men's Experiences of their own Fathers' in Nigel Beail and Jacqueline McGuire (eds.), *Fathers: Psychological Perspectives*, Junction Books, 1982.

9   Missing Mothers: The Effects of Women Working

Lynette Burrows

1   Summary and Introduction

Contemporary society is dismissive or derogatory of those women who remain at home to bring up their children. It assumes that what they do is easy, even unnecessary, and accord it little prestige. Yet the evidence shows that early learning and development of character are crucial to children's overall education. It is, above all, the continual presence of a mother who loves and is loved which provides the stimulus and patterns to make this learning possible. Society should take much more seriously the caring maternal role and its schools should provide some of the practical training which is necessary to run a home. Fortunately its dismissive attitude is likely to do less harm in the future as changes in employment patterns make it easier for women to retain a substantial commitment to the home.

2   Society's derogatory attitude to 'housewives'

Let us start with three common, sexist propositions. The first is that every woman who works at home is a prisoner and every man who has a job is a free agent. The second is that, if a man studies an academic subject like Classics or Medieval French and then becomes a civil servant, he is held to be doing very well for himself whereas if a woman studies English or Modern Languages and then becomes a mother she is thought to be wasting her education. The third is that if a man occupies his own premises, organises his work and begins an enterprise, it is called 'being his own boss'. Whereas if a woman does the same thing it is called 'being stuck at home' and everyone feels sorry for her.

There can only be one explanation for the widespread and derogatory attitudes embodied in these propositions and that is that the work women do in the home is intrinsically unnecessary and superfluous and that it cannot be done well. Hence the organs which carry educated or fashionable opinion to the public at large conduct a campaign of remorseless pity for the poor housewife to the extent that even women who are perfectly content in the role find themselves embarrassed and ashamed to admit that they are 'only a housewife'.

Sometimes this superior pity is of the overtly bracing kind, as from a Tory councillor recently; 'The trouble with too many women is that they get stuck at home bringing-up children when they could be using their talents pursuing careers in local administration'.

More often the invitation to pity is of a more subversive and cloying kind implying but not describing someone inept who is waiting to be helped at home. Typical of this formula is a recent 'Woman's Hour' interview in which a top chef was asked about his work. After talking at length about his job supervising and preparing food, the interviewer asked him accusingly whether he ever helped his wife with her work at home. The poor man, cornered by more unspoken, accumulated feminist propaganda than he knew how to handle, blustered defensively for a while before lapsing into lame excuses about not having much time. The truth of his situation was just as likely to have been that his wife, being a robust Latin like himself, neither needed nor wanted his help but ran a home that was as skillfully managed as his job. Furthermore that she would no more have expected him to help her than he would have welcomed her turning up at his hotel on a similar mission of mercy. The fact that this possibility was not even contemplated by either side in the interview is a sign of the cultural clout carried by the negative view of the housewife and of how weak has been any opposition to it.

Pity must be one of the easiest emotions to conjure up and, like pessimism, it seldom goes very deep particularly when it is brandished merely as a weapon with which to make others feel uncomfortable. Consequently, we should not be surprised that we are so often made aware, by concern on the media, of such problems as neglected infants, latch-key children, non-articulate primary school children, ten year old glue-sniffers and pubescent delinquents whilst, at the same time, the people who might have been able to solve their problems – their mothers – have been demoralized in the home and encouraged to get out of by the same media people pitying them for lack of personal fulfilment.

It is also a curious thing that, despite the many books and articles on child-care, we do not seem to take seriously the idea that there is such a thing as good and responsible mothering with certain specific requirements which cannot be successfully avoided or delegated.

3   Importance of mother in educating children from birth to five years

The education of children, in its full sense, is recognised by all psychologists to begin at birth. That is why in the United States they have developed special programmes to try to improve the performance of disadvantaged children at school. They were often found to be behind other children even by the time they started pre-school education at three and a half and the programme aims to help them by helping their mothers talk to and relate to their children from birth.

Few people with experience of children will be surprised at this obvious piece of common sense since no-one can have failed to notice what a phenomenal amount of learning has taken place in the period from birth to school age. What is more, the things that have been learnt are not confined to the more academic areas of speech, concept-forming and cognitive ability. They include such vital areas as a child's self-confidence and sense of humour, optimism, curiosity, response to discipline and concern for others. Children of only three years old show marked differences in the development of all these qualities and most of the difference comes from the way they have been brought up.

No child is born either good or bad; they are morally neutral. They *learn* to be good, just as they learn to be bad from the way they are treated and taught. All children are born with a 'self' – that much is very apparent; and so the possibility that they will become 'selfish' is always present. They are led out of this limiting, destructive tendency primarily by means of their love for another person, their mother. Their love for her is the basis for concern and interest in others because, starting with her, it gradually widens to include all the people with whom they share their lives.

I suppose it could be considered a misfortune that all children who are born need and love their mothers passionately since it is not always the case that their mothers feel the same about them. However, since it is an instinct in babies to feel like that about their mothers I should have thought that any society that was genuinely interested in the well-being of its children would have done more than we do to acknowledge and emphasise the fact lest, by default, it should go unremarked.

Such is the nature of man's wayward ingenuity, it has always been possible to distort or ignore even the most natural and free-flowing emotions. Spartan women were taught not to cry if their husbands or lovers were killed in war but to rejoice instead at their honour. Their mothers too were persuaded into making stern statements to their sons leaving for battle, to the effect that they had better come back either victorious or dead! Similarly, at odd periods of our history it has been the fashion to regard babies as rather unclean and to give them to poor working women to breast-feed whilst their mothers, presumably, struggled with hot compresses and bandages to stem the natural flow of their own milk.

Nor were these perverse digressions from natural behaviour without their effects. Sparta, under her unnatural regime, lost all of her former artistic and creative ability and became wholly militaristic. As for the children of those fashion-following ladies who employed a wet-nurse, few have left any testimony about their psychological state more clearly, if unwittingly, than the great and good Samuel Johnson. He suffered all his life from scrofula and blindness contracted from his wet-nurse but he could never explain or understand his own periods of blank depression and apathy or the fact that he never learnt to respect his mother although he loved her. Had he had children of his own, he might have observed, in the intimacy of his home, how uniquely capable and impressive women are as mothers to their young children. And also how infrequently one ever sees them anywhere else in such an unrivalled and commanding light.

It does not matter that the child may later grow to be more intellectual or more gifted than the mother. The fact that, during their formative years, she was to them the all-powerful lover and law-giver who satisfied their every need when she fed and loved them, leaves its imprint on them forever. Their love for her, plus their admiration for everything she represents coalesce into a respect that has been a central, if unacknowledged, part of the relationship between men and women in our culture.

When women do not fulfil this largely unremembered but deeply felt role to their babies, the child grows up to see its mother un-avoidably in a different light. Like Dr. Johnson they love them but they assess them more coolly as just one of a range of people who serviced their early lives and they never seem to lose a vague sense of loss and resentment which haunts many moods in later life.

4   Natural love of mother and child

Our version of this kind of cultural aberration is, I believe, our refusal to face and discuss the implications of babies having a seri-ous love for their mothers. All such aberrations have a reason and it may safely be concluded that our unwillingness to confront this fact is because to acknowledge it would be to 'tie women down' to being at home; whereas we prefer to see them tied down to a job in a factory or office. We are like someone who starts up a passionate love-affair with another and then, when they are hooked, severely limits their access to ourselves. Only in this case the unfairness is doubled since the poor lover is young and inexperienced and, what is more, cannot *speak* to plead his cause or voice his misery.

It is not a question of women not loving their children or of being indifferent to them. Most parents love their children with all their hearts; but *culturally* we simply have not considered that the love is mutual and what, therefore, it means to a baby to be given to others to be looked after. I had no idea myself when I first began baby-minding despite the fact that I already had six children of my own all under the age of eleven. Only the baby was left at home by then with all the others at school or playgroup and it seemed a good idea to make a little money by looking after other people's babies. Two or three make very little difference when you are already look-ing after one.

At least, it made very little difference to me but it made a lot of difference to them. They hated being left and made no attempt to disguise the fact, screaming and crying at every parting for many days and even weeks. Finally, when they realized that their crying was not going to achieve the function for which it was designed – to alert their mothers to their distress and bring her to them – they would lapse into querulous and fitful sleep to shut out the misery.

It was very shocking to me because, when you know how robustly cheerful and full of interest a baby of only a few months old is when he is secure and content, it is disturbing to see them so unhappy. Instead of the cheery, communicative gurgles and vigorous arm-waving of a baby happily amusing himself in his mother's company, there was the whimpering sleep or distracted gaze of a baby desperate for a sight or sound of the only face and form that would give it comfort.

It was not nearly so bad if the mother was only away for three or four hours because they quickly became aware of the routine and would simply lose themselves in sleep to kill the time and that helped to make them more cheerful. Nevertheless, the moment the footfall sounded in the hall, or at the merest whisper of the loved voice, they would start up and almost levitate out of the cradle and into their mother's arms.

And what would I say in reply to the anxious inquiry; 'How's she been?' Well, I would say what I guess all baby-minders say; 'Oh, fine! she's been asleep most of the time and only cried for ten minutes after you left.' This simple, factual explanation may have been alright for the mothers who only worked part-time because they had the rest of the day and the evenings to spend with the child, to get to know it. But I have often thought since that the mothers who left their children with me all day to sleep and brood probably had no idea of what would normally go on between a mother and her child in the course of a day and what the child gets from it.

Babies are not thinkers. They do not sit around pondering upon life's problems or remembering the past; they have nothing much to think about. They are either awake and *learning* or they are asleep. Nothing that happens anywhere around a waking baby goes unnoticed. Not a person comes in nor a sound is heard, nor a shadow flits across the wall but the baby notices it and files it away in its mind. Life is to them composed entirely of significant experiences; of emotions felt, expressed and shaped by how they are received; of interest aroused and satisfied; of an instinct to communicate and to understand that is painstakingly practised for every waking minute. So exhausting is all this for them that they drop into sleep like little animals the moment they are tired and need a rest.

You can select any little cameo you like from the course of a normal day and examine it in more detail and you will see the significance of the relationship between the baby and its mother. She may be just doing her work, perhaps thinking of other things, but the baby is learning lessons all the time. For example, his mother is sewing and listening to the radio, tapping her foot. He is sitting on the floor among the fragments of material which he picks up and examines. Some are long so they trail on the floor, some short so they wave in the air; he tries it several times to test the consistency. He listens to the music and watches his mother's mouth as she sings in unison. He opens his own voice in discordant accompaniment and it pleases him that he can produce a sound so similar.

His mother drops a little piece of cloth on his head and laughs at him. Full of excitement, he feels carefully up the side of his head not knowing where the top is. He finds it with a look of concentration on his face and locates the material which he pulls off and dashes to the ground with a triumphant cry.

When he has turned over and moved all the large objects around him he will concentrate on even the tiniest fragments of cloth on the floor; picking them up with fingers as delicate as a little capuchin monkey's and practising the movement over and over. He holds each one out, abruptly, to his mother who accepts them without stopping her work but only saying 'Taa' which he repeats gravely to himself in different tones of voice. In fact he keeps up the babbling talk most of the time and his mother talks in return. They are not exactly talking *to* each other but they are talking together and very soon the baby can imitate the very pitch and tone of proper speech even without the vocabulary.

And so it goes on throughout the day, with meals and naps, cuddles and walks to vary still more the range of delights. It does not last long, this baby-hood; two or three years and it is all gone, with the sturdy child well set on the road to independence. But they have an instinct to protest about being pushed out too early before all the learning and feeling has been integrated into a harmonious and untroubled self.

5   Educative power of love

It was only the experience of having a couple of children all day that really drew my attention to how comparatively vacuous and under-functioning babies are without their mothers. These children could not take refuge in wall-to-wall sleep since the time was just too long so they had to soldier on through all the weary hours until their mothers reappeared.

Their reactions were of course mixed but could mostly be summed up in the word *desultory*. They did nothing with any enthusiasm or real enjoyment and seldom initiated either talk or activity. There was something so definitely lacking in their response to everything as compared to an ordinary child with its mother that one could not fail to notice it.

On summer days I would pack the two or three children into the big pram and cross the road into the Botanic Gardens where we would play on the grass and feed the birds. It was there that I finally identified the missing ingredient as love. It was not 'baby love' or 'maternal love'; or any other kind of qualified love. It was love pure and simple. The same kind that makes a long walk seem short, a dingy cinema glamorous and the merest activity seem worthwhile and interesting if it is done by two people who love one another.

With a child it is not a sexual love of course, but it is physical and the amount of kissing and cuddling that goes on is comparable to what we put into relationships later on. The practical result is that you do so much more for each other and make so much more effort with everything when you first come to love someone in this way.

The baby makes an effort to learn in order to please and to come closer to his mother. She unconsciously teaches him by all the manifestations of her love; playing, singing, being amused by antics and impressed by progress. Nothing is ever much of a bore when it is done in that atmosphere, which must be why we spend most of our lives trying to find love and to keep it.

Even that humble walk in the park to sit in the sun and do nothing in particular becomes especially enjoyable when it is done with someone you love. As an adult, one has to cast one's mind back to those early days of romance and to the hours spent watching an adored boyfriend greasing a filthy motorbike in a freezing garage to remember the power of new love to make everything special.

This experience of new love is the same for a baby as it is for a young person or an adult. It is also the same for the mother if she gives it a chance to develop rather than curtailing it by going back to work and leaving her child. It is very catching and I truly believe that many parents learn it from their babies and not the other way round.

It is a time when the emotions have a chance to grow and mature because they have been awakened by love. Care, concern, interest, subtlety, sympathy; they all arise first out of this love and, if exercised freely and without anxiety, settle happily into the child's personality. It does seem that we ignore this early love and its educative power over our emotions perhaps because, by the time we *could* express it, we have forgotten its details.

However, even if everyone were to accept as a fact that babies and children love and need their mothers, there would still be two major factors conspiring to push women back to work after having their babies. One is that they need the money and the other is that they are afraid they will be bored at home with only a child for company.

6   Training necessary to run a home

As I have said above, motherhood has not had a good 'press' for a long time and women could be forgiven for thinking that the home has nothing to offer them but servitude and gloom. However, there has been an increasing awareness over the years of some of the drawbacks of a home and children without adequate supervision or attention from the mother. Perhaps the time is ripe to suggest that a different, more positive approach to home life should be openly embraced; particularly in schools which could do so much.

I well remember quitting the job-scene after my second child was born having continued to teach part-time with the first. Needing money as all young families do, I had started a playgroup in a local hall with a friend who had two children of the same age as mine. We gathered around us a whole collection of other young mothers of widely different backgrounds to help run the playschool and to raise money for our various ambitious schemes.

There we were, in a predictable period of our lives, looking after our young children just as 90 per cent of girls say they want to do. So how had our education helped us? We must have had about five hundred years of expensive education between us and yet there were few, if any, who had learnt any useful home skills at school. We had all learnt how to make a macaroni cheese and that is about all. None of us, for example, had learnt how to make bread and that probably summed up our deficiencies – they were basic. Then and now, girls were given a mock-training for normal domestic life that is quite scandalously unimaginative and inadequate. My own daughter recently had to make a Quiche in her 'Home Economics' class that required a pound of mushrooms and a pint of double cream!

The trouble is that educationists have not given sufficient thought to the kind of practical knowledge and information that a girl needs if she wants to run an interesting and productive home. If she does not go out to work she will have more time than most for planning and carrying out paid work at home and she needs information about this just as she needs advice about economies that can be made when you have the opportunity to make more of your own requirements than is usual today.

One sees the educationists' problem. There are not too many teachers who have sufficient knowledge and experience of home life to know what to teach and how; but this obstacle is not insurmountable. One of the improvements that an enlightened Head of Domestic Science could make would be to invite knowledgeable and experienced housewives into the schools to demonstrate their skills. How the style and atmosphere of these lessons would improve from the rather dowdy image they have now if they comprised such subjects as the brewing of ale and making country wines. How to make cosmetics and shampoos, and save pounds;

and how to prepare and administer herbal remedies and 'medicinal compounds'.

Educationally all these subjects have impeccable credentials. They involve practical knowledge of nature and natural science, nutrition and chemistry and they could not be said to be beneath the intelligence of even the ablest student.

Turning to the more academic side, again the deficiencies in our approach to giving girls a relevant education weigh principally against those who might want to work at home. Children are taught how to pass exams and how to get a job and that is about all. A more realistic approach for girls contemplating marriage and mother-hood would be to include some talks and advice on how to adapt a typical career so that it could be continued from home or on a part-time basis.

It would also be very useful if, alongside all the 'civic studies' and sociology, they could learn how to set up and run a co-operative, so at least they would be able to buy foodstuffs and materials cheaply with other housewives for their own use and for any enterprise they might want to start. Girls are far more likely to be their own bossess, at least for a time, than boys and there should be some element in the education system which takes account of this.

7 More flexibility in work and domestic roles

For the rest, probably things are moving in the direction of the housewife anyway. As the industrial job scene contracts and more people buy their own homes where they can live and work if they want to, more people are going to be engaged in home-centred activities than has been usual in the post-war generation when everyone went out of the home for everything.

We have always had a home-centred ideal inside of us anyway. Proverbs about homes being castles, and no places being like it, abound and we have never given up the right to have a little piece of garden each, even on an island as small as ours. There is no doubt that if such a revolution does come about it will be a good thing for children – and for many women.

One thing is certain, homes are always ruled by women in a way that few other places ever are. So, if one is going to have a ruling class, it is surely a matter for rejoicing that it should be so democratically distributed throughout the whole community.

10   Should Sons and Daughters be Brought Up Differently?: Radical Feminism in Schools

Mervyn Hiskett

1   Summary and Introduction

Parents have traditionally entertained rather different expectations of their sons and daughters. Currently they are under pressure to change these traditional expectations especially where girls are concerned and the pressure comes from radical feminists who are adamant that daughters must not be brought up for female roles. It is sometimes exerted directly on parents but, more often, it is directed at schools, trying to persuade them to change the way they treat girl pupils. Parents are expected to co-operate with these changes.

In fact, parents would do well to think hard about the changes sought by the feminists both at home and school and to question the assumptions behind them, for they are extremely doubtful. To illustrate such assumptions, this chapter subjects one particular document to scrutiny, *Equal opportunities and the school governor* published by the Equal Opportunities Commission (EOC),[1] and examines, one by one, the main feminist premises put forward in this document as well as the ways in which the radical feminists seek to impose them. First, the assertion that the perceived differences between men and women are not the result of real factors but are due simply to 'stereotyping'.

2   'Manliness' and 'womanliness' stereotyping or the facts of economic life?

At page seven of the pamphlet the authors make the following keynote statement:

At present boys and girls do not, in a number of important respects, receive equal benefit from their schooling, largely because of stereotypical attitudes about male and female roles...Such attitudes are present on a massive scale in the wider society outside the school.

But what do the feminists mean by stereotyping which, they claim, is 'present on a massive scale in the wider society'? A moment's thought will make it clear that what they are expressing in strongly pejorative terms can equally well be described in quite different language – namely that a great many people, almost certainly a majority, in the Western world, have certain ideals of manliness and womanhood inherited from their parents and grandparents, which they cherish as part of their culture, and which they have found serve society well in establishing relationships of courtesy, mutual respect and consideration among men and women.

Why, then, should they abandon these traditional attitudes, either as regards their own behaviour or in the matter of bringing up their children, and replace them with untried feminist notions which do not have the support of inherited wisdom and experience behind them? But the issue goes beyond biological and cultural considerations alone. For when it comes to career differences, we now know that these differences are not between men and women, as the feminists insist, but between married women with families and everyone else. Sowell has shown, 'The median annual income of women has generally fluctuated...at a level just under three-fifths of that of men'[2] and radical feminists have latched onto this bald statistic as proof that women are discriminated against. But a little reflection makes it clear that the great majority of women in our society either are, or will become married; and married women are, overwhelmingly, part-time workers because they usually either opt out of work altogether for a period of years in order to bring up a family, or they reduce their working hours for the same reason. Thus, inevitably, there is a wage cost. But there is also an experience cost because a married woman lawyer, for example, misses some years of practical experience in court, a married woman academic misses some research experience, and so on. This, again inevitably, has a cost in promotion prospects, especially in the professions and the higher ranks of business.

However, if we consider the case of unmarried women, the position is entirely different. For unmarried women earn, on average, 91 per cent of the income of single men. This alone, is enough to cast doubt on the extreme feminist claim that women, as women, are discriminated against. The missing 9 per cent is, of course, largely accounted for by unwed motherhood, for unmarried women who bear children are subject to much the same economic restraints as married women.[3]

Yet another important statistic shows that married men earn, on average, more than single men and enjoy better promotion prospects. The reason for this is that they tend to have more time to devote to career building, and are probably more highly motivated, especially if they have children. But this higher income of the married man ought to be regarded as a joint income, for the wife obviously makes an important contribution to earning it, and also benefits from it in several obvious ways, not least of which, in the UK, is that this joint income pays a mortgage on a house that is normally jointly owned. So even during those periods of her life when a married woman is not in any form of paid employment, it is doubtful whether she is seriously disadvantaged economically, except of course if the husband acts unfairly. But that is a personal matter that has individual remedies.

To repeat Sowell's neat observation, 'The big difference is not between men and women but between married women and everybody else'.[4] So the career differences between men and women, boys and girls, are certainly not due to something irrational called stereotyping. They are due to the influence which the institution of marriage exerts on the economic life of our society and they can only be changed by changing that institution. Parents are naturally and properly aware of these economic realities which radical feminists choose to ignore; and the advice that they customarily give their children sensibly takes into account the fact that boys will normally have a whole working life to devote to career building, while girls will normally devote a part of their lives to child-rearing. To ignore these realities, as the radical feminists want us to do, would be irresponsible, for it would in many cases lead children, especially girls, to take early career decisions without understanding that they might subsequently conflict with their wish to marry and raise a family. Of course, if girls decide, none the less, to choose such careers in full awareness of the possible consequences, they have every right to do so, but it is the duty of parents and teachers to make sure that they are indeed aware of these and not to pretend that the problem does not exist, which is what these feminists are, in effect, asking both parents and teachers to do.

But there is another way in which radical feminists seek to lead parents by the nose when they suggest that to advise children to choose careers according to their gender is 'stereotyping'. For they fail to make it clear that to discriminate on the ground of sex is only wrong when and in so far as sex is not properly relevant. But when it is relevant, there is a positive duty to discriminate. For example, it would be unreasonable to advise a girl against becoming a doctor simply on the ground that the person advising her preferred, personally, to be treated by male doctors. But it would not be wrong to advise her against choosing a career as a meat porter or a night-club bouncer. Nor would it be wrong to point out to her that in seeking to become a site foreman, she was entering a predominantly male occupation where she might find difficulty in asserting her authority. In the first example the advice is based on nothing more substantial than personal preference. In the second and third examples it rests on mature experience indicating that only a tiny proportion of women are happy in such occupations. In other words, it rests on inherited wisdom which parents have accumulated over generations of care and concern for children. To deny a place to inherited wisdom, which in effect is what the EOC and the more extreme feminists are urging the rest of us to do, is to deny the duty of adults to counsel the young.

3   Radical feminists attempt to replace traditional assumptions

The authors of the EOC pamphlet write:

> …many girls and boys choose certain options and reject others on the basis of conformity to what is expected of a pupil of their sex rather than on the basis of interest and aptitude. Their choices are thus not real choices but reactions to direct and indi-

rect pressures and may be regretted in the future, when it is too late.[5]

Of course, life is full of decisions that are regretted when it is too late. But it is absurd to suggest, as the EOC does here, that regretted or unfortunate choices are necessarily not real or genuine choices. The fact is, all of life is a response to pressures of one sort or the other and it is intellectually dishonest to pretend that there is ever a situation when a choice can be made in a total vacuum. At best, all they are seeking to do is to replace one set of pressures – traditional and sometimes conservative ones – with a different set of progressivist ones. But there is no reason to suppose that the latter will be more productive of human happiness and fulfilment than the former. This can be illustrated by the following examples. A girl wishes to train as an airline pilot but is persuaded against this by her parents, who honestly believe that this is not a suitable career for a girl, and particularly not for their daughter whose temperament they believe to be unsuited to it, and they persuade her to work in a bank instead. The girl complies but continues to regret what she feels to have been a lost opportunity. Another girl, the daughter of a family with progressive views, is persuaded by her ardently feminist mother not to go straight into nursing, which would have been her own choice, but to go on to university and qualify as a civil engineer, a career for which her mother feels she has the intellectual potential. This she does, to the delight of the mother, who regards her achievement as a step on the way to realising the radical feminist vision. But the girl, who is indeed intellectually able but of a shy and retiring disposition, finds that she has entered a male-dominated profession and, because she experiences great difficulty in making her authority felt in the field, ends up spending more and more of her time doing paper work in an office. She becomes unhappy and frustrated in consequence and regrets that she was persuaded against becoming a nurse. Both girls have been subject to pressures and have made choices that 'are regretted afterwards'. Concerning the first case, we may be sure that radical feminists would wax mightily indignant. About the second case, it is doubtful whether they would have a word to say!

There is, of course, no absolute solution to the problem that parents may sometimes be wrong. But the greatest hope of avoiding this lies in their individual concern for their children, their readiness to talk with them and also to take a plurality of advice – from teachers, career advisors, their friends in business and the professions – and then to frame their own independent advice to their children, not according to some egalitarian principle but in the light of their knowledge of the child's total personality, of which gender certainly forms a part.

4   How unequal are opportunities?

According to some feminists, boys and girls can only choose careers 'on the basis of interest and aptitude' if they are prepared to fly in the face of 'conformity to what is expected of a pupil of their sex'.[6] But this is surely contradicted by the reality that we all see around us. Such vocational roles as doctor, surgeon, company director, investment manager, insurance salesperson, barrister, solicitor, member of the armed forces, policewoman, accountant, civil servant, physicist, pharmacist, university don, Minister of State, Prime Minister, train driver, bus driver and so on, *ad infinitum*, are filled by women none of whom seem to have had to face insuperable obstacles of prejudice and 'stereotyping' in order to get there. So why is it necessary to maintain a quango, at the public expense, and to waste school time on extreme feminist propaganda, to achieve what society has so obviously already conceded – freedom for women to enter virtually any profession or occupation they wish? The fact is that despite some conservative resistance that ought to be regarded as a healthy braking influence, womens' emancipation has already been achieved as a result of powerful but impersonal social forces, in particular those generated by two world wars. This spontaneous process is largely benign because it is in tune with what society requires and is able to tolerate. But extreme feminist pressure groups and apparently the EOC are not content with this. They seek, for ideological reasons, to push the process even further, beyond the point that most people think necessary or desirable.

5   Radical feminists seek to achieve aims through interference in education

Unfortunately, the activities of such pressure groups have a distorting influence on what goes on in schools. As Digby Anderson points out in a recent article in *The Times*,[7] it is a characteristic of our society that many people will conform to certain progressivist patterns of behaviour simply out of fear that they may otherwise be thought reactionary. This is all the more so when their own career prospects depend on gaining and keeping the approval of progressivist superiors. Many school governors and parents who are of a conservative turn of mind, will be uncomfortably familiar with the head teacher who shows them round the school and proudly points to the number of girls doing 'boy' subjects and boys doing 'girl' subjects. Now there is nothing wrong in a girl doing metalwork and a boy doing domestic science if, in each case, the individual pupil genuinely wants to do the subject. But what is wrong is that undue persuasion should be used to bring this about. It does seem however that this is sometimes the case and that schools will deliberately encourage girls to take 'boy' subjects and vice versa, simply in order to massage the figures and satisfy HM Inspectors that 'equal opportunities' policies are being implemented.

The same progressivist tendency to manipulate influences the conduct of sport in state schools. For instance, the present writer recalls the case of a mother at a primary school parents' meeting some years ago, who complained that her little boy constantly came home from school crying because he and his friends were made to do needlework during activity periods, when what they wanted to do was play football. The mother felt this to be wrong and had the courage to stand up and say so. The response from the teachers represented at the meeting was frigid. It was baldly stated that nobody on the staff was qualified to coach and referee football, a very lame excuse when it was simply a case of supervising a group of little boys who wanted to play at football by kicking a ball around. It therefore seems likely that the school, for other reasons, preferred the boys to do needlework.

A similar example of the absurd lengths to which feminist enthusiasm can go when it is let loose in schools is that of a lady who made a great fuss because girls in the school in which she was interested, were not actively encouraged to play cricket as fellow members of the same team with boys. It was in vain that the head teacher pointed out that girls were free to play cricket if they wanted to but in fact none of them did. Nothing would satisfy this ardent feminist short of an assurance that active steps would be taken to 'encourage' girls to play cricket in mixed teams with boys – that is, they would be pressured into doing so. Yet such a procedure is not only absurdly time wasting; it also completely misses the point of physical education, the purpose of which is to help young people to develop their full physical potential, train them in healthy living habits, help them to experience the joy of vigorous physical exercise and to cultivate the team spirit. All of these objectives are just as well, if not better served through such games as lacrosse, netball, hockey, tennis and so on, which are traditionally played by girls, than they are through cricket which, whatever its other virtues, is not distinguished by vigorous exercise. What, therefore, is the point of insisting that girls join the boys' cricket teams? The answer appears to be that certain feminists regard it as a symbol of the triumph of their ideas. Such posturing wastes time that would be better spent on more useful conventional activities.

A further example of feminist extremism in education will be found in the GCSE Social Studies syllabus of the Southern Examining Group for 1988. This syllabus presents a Specimen Examination Paper, Question 9 of which requires candidates to 'study the pictures below and answer the questions which follow'. The first of the two pictures, labelled 1950, shows three little boys paddling in the sea and playing with boats, while a little girl sits on the beach playing with her doll. The second picture, labelled 1970, shows a small boy of 'Just William' age but sanitized appearance, engaged in the improbable task of flower arranging with a little girl who, it would be nice to think, represents a reformed Violet Elizabeth Bott! Candidates have to answer a number of questions based on these pictures, one of which is 'Men and women are still unequal today. Why do you think this is the case?' As is made clear above, this statement is based on a misreading of the career statistics of men and women, and is in any case not born out by observations of the vocational roles that women actually fill. Yet children are taught this nonsense and even their school-leaving examinations are turned into vehicles for radical feminist propaganda.

Another case of extreme feminist ideology seeping through into the national school examination system is to be detected in an official publication of the University of London School Examinations Board (ULSEB),[8] a venerable and hitherto respected academic institution that now seems to have fallen into the hands of the brave new-worlders. The publication is intended in the first instance for the guidance of examiners, but it will, of course, be read and applied by teachers preparing pupils for ULSEB examinations, including the new GCSE. Under the section heading 'Sexism and language' the anonymous authors recommend the avoidance of what they call 'sex-specific forms' and the substitution of 'neutral terms'. Thus, to use their own examples, we may no longer say or write 'the psychologist…he…' but must turn this on its back in such a way as to avoid the allegedly 'sexist' implication. Nor, yet more absurdly, may we say or write, 'Research scientists often neglect their wives and children' since this gives the game away by indicating that the research scientists are male – a subtle affront, so the authors apparently believe, to women! After further solemn deliberation upon the relative merits and demerits of such forms as 's/he' and 'he/she', these latter-day scholastics go on to recommend what seem to me clumsy circumlocutions in order to avoid the trauma to the hyper-sensitive radical feminist sensibility of discovering that it was born into a world where, as far as I know, no language has a singular unisex, as opposed to a singular impersonal ('it') pronoun and where, therefore, the artist, the politician, the con man, the concert pianist *et al.*, have all been referred to generically as 'he' since human speech began.

I accept that, by the standards that prevail among those who compiled this ULSEB pamphlet, such manhandling – or ought one to write wo/manhandling? – of language is necessary in order to avoid what they genuinely see as unfairness to, or even deliberate discrimination against women. But just because they honestly think this, it is no reason why it should be taken on by the rest of us as gospel and imposed on children through the state examination system. For there is another point of view that the authors of the ULSEB pamphlet choose to ignore – namely that an indeterminate number of women are certainly not offended, or even marginally concerned by the fact that the masculine singular pronoun is used as a generic reference (the injustice is, of course, removed at a stroke once we move into the plural!), that they habitually use it themselves in this way without giving the matter a thought and that, if they were asked to give an opinion about it, they would reply that the whole argument is extremely trivial and not worth wasting time on. In my opinion that indeterminate number represents an overwhelming majority. The authors of the pamphlet are, of course, entitled to disagree.

But there is another, rather more serious objection to the adoption of such attitudes in the national examination system. It is that if such pettifogging faddism is allowed to gain ground in schools, the result will surely be to rear a whole generation of ideological cranks whose sense of values will be no better than those of the GLC councillors described by Anne Sofer, for whom

> ...it becomes far more important to introduce non-sexist language into the committee than to see that any individual woman has her roof repaired.[9]

6 What kind of society do parents want for their children?

> ...all pupils should leave school as well prepared as possible given their different abilities, to achieve financial independence...Their sex should not be allowed to get in the way of these objectives.[10]

No reasonable person is likely to quarrel with the view that girls as well as boys should be so educated that they are capable of becoming financially independent should the need arise. All the same, it is surely obvious that the out-and-out female careerism and the search for independence at all costs, which is what the extreme feminists appear to be advocating, must sooner or later reach the point where it becomes incompatible with the continued existence of the nuclear family in its present form. Indeed that point may already have been reached. For one of the more disturbing trends in present-day society is the increase in such social phenomena as 'Dinkyism' (Double-income-no-kids), an unduly prolonged state of childlessness during which both partners work full time and post-pone starting a family, which is generally agreed to be one of the causes of the increase in early divorce.

To push this process yet further, as these feminists so obviously wish to do, is bound to entail yet more disruptive social consequences. For the total, life-long financial independence for women that is the radical feminist goal, must necessarily involve all of the individual's time and effort. It cannot be done on a part-time basis. The only way in which this inescapable economic fact can be reconciled with child rearing is by a major extension of crèche facilities. Indeed, radical feminist lobbies have been agitating for years for just such a development, provided, needless to say by the state. Thus the outcome of such forward feminist policies, if they are successful, will be crèchism on the scale that was tried, but later abandoned in Israel but which has become a permanent institution in the USSR. And, as part and parcel of such a development, one may confidently expect a considerable increase in what is already widely recognised as a social evil – the institution of the one-parent family. For women who have been brought up to regard total financial independence as the main goal in life will inevitably hesitate about a commitment to marriage. The implications of such developments for the society of the future are grave indeed. Parents have a moral duty to consider carefully what the feminist zealots are working to bring about, whether deliberately or because of a lack of understanding and foresight; and to decide whether or not they wish to go along with it.

Of course, many out-and-out feminists will argue that such difficulties can be avoided if only men would take over what these feminists consider to be their fair share of child rearing and thus free women to be bread winners. And they will also argue that the manpower requirements of a modern economy are such that the full-time participation of women as workers is essential. But these are hollow arguments. In the first place, it is surely obvious that not all men are going to be willing to relinquish their traditional roles, however much some feminists press for them to do so. Therefore, if the institution of marriage in its present already somewhat attenuated form, is to survive, not all women can have full-time careers. Second, suppose that roles were to become completely reversed, as radical feminists want them to be, how would this help the economy? Whereas in the past, x number of men worked and y number of women stayed at home to bring up the children, under the feminist dispensation, x number of women would work and y number of men would stay at home. So where is the economic gain?

None the less, the radical feminist vision can indeed be achieved (although the reality might turn out to be no more pleasing to the feminists themselves than to the rest of society) but only if parents and potential parents totally abdicate their responsibility for rearing children within individual families and farm them out to crèches run by the state or by some other vast impersonal organisation. Those who recoil from such a blueprint for the future would be well advised to take a stand against attempts by extreme feminist organisations to introduce into the national education system, by stealth and by moral bullying, provisions that can only result in bringing this about.

7   Radical feminists seek removal of 'sexist' books from school libraries

One of the most unpleasant aspects of extremist feminist activity, which is advocated by the EOC[11] is book censorship. The EOC provides school governors with a 'Checklist for Action', the purpose of which is to detect and eliminate from reading and teaching materials all that is sexist. But it is necessary to understand what ideological feminists mean by 'sexist' for the word has nothing to do with sexuality, physical lust, the libido or whatever. Nor are these feminists railing against page three of *The Sun*. Indeed, many of them express indifference to, or even approval of the commercial exploitation of sex, which they believe can be turned to their purpose. What 'sexist' means in the feminist ideological lexicon is anything that differentiates men from women. Thus feminists of advanced views have, from time to time, objected to such literary classics as *Pride and Prejudice*, on the ground that it portrays a society which accepted and even deliberately cultivated these differences – which is of course perfectly true, it did! Likewise; they have objected to Thomas Hardy's *Tess of the Durbervilles*, and have taken exception to a long list of childrens' story books stretching from the Victorian era down to more recent times. Thus H. Rider Haggard, the author of *She* and other boys' adventure stories, Rudyard Kipling, J.M. Barrie, author of *Peter Pan*, Baroness Orczy, author of *The Scarlet Pimpernel*, Richmal Crompton, author of the *Just William* series and, of course, Beatrix Potter, have all come under the radical feminist ban on the ground that, one way or the other, they perpetuate the traditional differences between boys and girls, whereas what such feminists seek is a childrens' literature that portrays flower arranging and playing with dolls, not train sets, as the proper pastimes for boys. As the pamphlet puts it, 'girls are regularly being shown in pictures helping mother indoors, while boys go out fishing with their fathers',[12] a complaint which, apart from its essential triviality, ignores the fact that girls, being on the whole instinctively more humane than boys, may have no wish to go fishing! Indeed the feminist activists have tried to create a whole new literature the sole purpose of which is to replace the traditional order of things with their own unnatural vision. For the pamphlet emphasises that 'non-sexist childrens' books are available, and school libraries could be encouraged to purchase these'.[13] Many parents may well feel that this obsession with changing childrens' established patterns of play is absurd. They may also agree with the present writer that to condemn an existing literature and to try to replace it with an alternative one, simply on ideological grounds, is an unpleasant manifestation of the totalitarian mind.

8   Radical feminist demands exceed the provisions of the law

At present the provision of equal opportunities for women is governed by the Sex Discrimination Act of 1975. While one may hold the opinion that the introduction of this Act in the first place was no more than a sop to progressive opinion, it is none the less the case that there is little about it that is objectionable as it has so far been interpreted and applied by the courts. Moreover, there is every indication that the great majority of people are content with the situation as it now stands. However, the more extreme feminists claim that the Act supports their demands and, in fact the EOC pamphlet is full of heavy-handed warnings that to fail to do as they demand puts one in danger of breaking the law.

The first comment to be made on all this is that such constant table thumping about the force of law is characteristic of frustrated zealots who turn to coercion in order to enforce what they are unable to gain by argument. This, of course, is the behaviour of authoritarians and totalitarians the world over and, as a wise lawyer has put it, 'The greatest dangers to liberty lurk in the insidious encroachment of men of zeal, well-meaning but without understanding'.[14] But radical feminists are in fact at times inconsistent in their appeal to the law. For while first claiming that we must all do as they demand because the law says so, they continue 'However, genuine equality of opportunity will not be achieved solely by basic compliance with the Act'[15] and then go on to advocate various kinds of radical feminist activism, the purpose of which is to advance the frontiers of the law beyond its present application. So they want it both ways. We are to obey the law by doing what they tell us to do. But we must also go beyond the law by doing what they tell us to do, and they insist that there is a 'collective responsibility' to do so. This is entirely unjustified. There is no responsibility, collective or individual, to go beyond the strict provision of the law as it at present stands. Nor is there any obligation on any school governor, parent or teacher to support such aims if he or she disagrees with them.

9   Parents should be alert to the attempt by feminists, to hijack their children

On the evidence of the EOC pamphlet, radical feminist assumptions are, broadly, that established differences between men and women, especially in relation to work, are the result of stereotyping; and that the traditional ideals of manliness and womanliness caused by this stereotyping ought to be overthrown by education, by the way in which parents bring up their children, by book censorship, by the deliberate manipulation of literature and so on. But such assumptions, to say nothing of the methods that go with them, are highly questionable and even objectionable. For the truth is that the differences that exist between men and women at work have been shown, in the great majority of cases, to be not the result of prejudice but of real factors foremost among which are the economic consequences of marriage and raising a family. These consequences cannot be changed except by drastically changing, and probably destroying the present family structure of our society which, of course, many feminists openly advocate.

Although the feminists claim they want children to have an unpressurised choice of career, this is in fact not true. What they really want is for them to be influenced by feminist criteria rather than traditional ones. While it is sensible to allow children of both sexes to have the widest possible choice of careers, it is also sensible that they be prepared for the sort of lives most of them will lead. Despite feminist arguments to the contrary, in the case of girls this means that marriage and the raising of a family ought to be taken fully into account as an option that the majority of them – over 90 per cent – are likely to choose.

Contrary to what the feminists wish us to believe, nothing is gained economically, morally or psychologically – and much is lost – by attempting to bring up boys as girls and girls as boys. Therefore, both at school and at home, parents should insist that due attention is given to fostering a boy's masculinity and a girl's femininity by making them aware of these aspects of their personalities and by encouraging them to engage in the kinds of activities that are traditionally associated with their gender, whether this be in the classroom, on the playing field or in their hobbies and leisure pursuits.

Notes and References

1. *Equal Opportunities and the School Governor*, EOC, February 1985.
2. Thomas Sowell, *Civil Rights: Rhetoric or Reality*, Basic Books, 1984,
3. Ibid., p. 92.
4. Ibid., p. 93.
5. *Equal Opportunities*, op. cit., p. 7.
6. Ibid.
7. Digby Anderson, 'The reluctant reactionaries', *The Times*, 28 October 19
8. *Sexism, Discrimination and Gender Biases in GCE Examinations*, ULS, March 1985.
9. *The Times*, 31 March 1986.
10. *Equal Opportunities*, op. cit., p. 7.
11. Ibid., pp. 17–19.
12. Ibid., p. 19.

13. Ibid.
14. Louis D. Brandeis, quoted in *The Times*, 14 July 1987.
15. *Equal Opportunities*, op. cit., p. 4.

11   The Rote Learning of Arithmetic

Gerry Mulhern

1   Summary and Introduction

> Whenever thought is necessary, it is to be expressed vigorously,
> but it should not be wasted over simple mechanical operations
> (Sir Oliver Lodge, *Easy Mathematics*)

During the hey-day of 'modern' mathematics in the 1960s and 1970s educators observed, not entirely tongue-in-cheek, that pupils knew that 7 × 6 was the same as 6 × 7, but they did not know that either was equal to 42! The somewhat apocryphal nature of this observation concealed a genuine anxiety amongst many educationists over the fundamental nature of 'modern' mathematics curricula. Sadly, in the wake of some 30 years of so-called 'new maths', it would appear that these fears were justified.

While, standards in mathematics teaching have been a source of concern to educators ever since the introduction of state education during the last century, this concern has reached unprecedented levels in recent years. Results of a survey of some 12,500 men and women born in 1958 (children of the 'new maths' era) suggest that as many as seven million people in the UK may be innumerate, illiterate, or both.[1] Furthermore, a recent survey by the National Foundation for Educational Research in England and Wales suggests that standards are continuing on a downward spiral, with an eight per cent fall in average achievement in mathematics of 13 and 14-year-olds between 1964 and 1981. The blame has been laid variously upon teachers, politicians, parents, examiners, curriculum planners, teacher-training colleges and universities. However, increasing numbers of educationists are beginning to acknowledge that some 30 years of teaching 'modern' mathematics has been responsible, at least in part, for producing a generation of mathematical incompetents.

So great has been government concern in recent years that in 1978 the Department of Education and Science commissioned a thorough review of mathematics education in the UK under the chairmanship of Sir William Cockcroft, the conclusions of which were published in 1982 in a 300-page document which has since become known as the 'Cockcroft Report'.[2]

Amongst the wide-ranging proposals of the report was the recommendation of a 'bottom-up' approach to mathematics teaching, whereby curricula should be seen to reflect the needs of the vast majority of pupils who leave school with little or no formal qualification in mathematics, rather than the five per cent of pupils who obtain an 'A' level pass in the subject. Paradoxically, however, the authors of the report rejected out of hand any suggestion of a 'back to basics' approach to mathematics teaching. This appears a bewildering decision which may add to the already parlous state of mathematics education in the UK.

2   Changing face of mathematics education: 'acquisition' in place of 'teaching'

It may be instructive at this juncture to consider briefly the factors which led to the introduction of modern mathematics in schools. During the 1950s many educators remarked that school mathematics was little different from that of the 1930s (an uncomfortable position for innovators of the day!), whereas, by contrast, university mathematics was undergoing wholesale change in response to burgeoning post-war technological advances in computing, operational research, linear programming, and the like. This state of affairs prompted many educationists to argue for change, if only for change's sake, and the subsequent surge of activity in curriculum development led to the introduction of so-called 'new' or 'modern' mathematics ('so-called' because most of the 'new' topics had their origins in the 18th century!).

Topics such as arithmetic, algebra and geometry were superseded by sets, topology, shape, symmetry, functions, relations, maps, vectors and matrices. In addition, educators proposed a vastly different style of teaching based principally on the ideas of Jean Piaget. Teachers no longer 'taught' mathematics. Instead, children were encouraged to 'acquire' understanding through practical experience, active participation, discovery and investigation, and pupils were encouraged to move freely about the classroom directing their own activities.

The 1950s and '60s became the era of 'blocks and rods'. During this time a host of didactical artefacts were introduced into the classroom at enormous cost to the taxpayer. Children were bombarded variously with Stern's blocks, Cuisenaire rods, Unifix blocks, Flavell's apparatus, and Deines' Multibase Arithmetic blocks. Researchers claimed that these appliances had two distinct advantages over traditional methods of instruction. Firstly, they were 'self-evident', whereas traditional symbolic manipulation (i.e. rote learning) was not, or so it was claimed. Secondly, they offered 'symbolic generality' (whatever that was!). In hindsight, it seems extraordinary that educators were prepared to subject a generation of schoolchildren to such a radical curriculum on such flimsy grounds.

3 Objections to rote learning are based on fashion rather than evidence

While it is beyond dispute that practical activity, discovery learning, exploration and investigation are enormously useful to pupils, what little evidence there is would suggest that these are of no benefit to young pre-numerate children. On the contrary, the fact that innumeracy is endemic amongst individuals who have been taught using these methods would suggest that they may well be harmful.

Perusal of the literature quickly leads one to conclude that at no point were traditional methods of teaching arithmetic, such as rote learning of arithmetic tables, found to be ineffective. Rather, researchers virtually without exception concluded that such learning was extremely beneficial for children of all levels of ability. Why, then, did rote learning meet so much opposition from the 1950s onwards? It would seem the problem was one of 'image' – learning by rote was simply unfashionable. There was a feeling amongst educationists that, somehow or other, rote learning of tables represented an infringement of children's civil liberties! Opponents rarely used the term 'rote', preferring instead more value-laden terms such as 'meaningless drill', 'mechanical learning' and 'authoritarian methods'.

Inevitably, arguments against rote learning of arithmetic tended to consist of a series of somewhat rash accusations, rather than coherent rebuttals based on empirical evidence. This was aptly illustrated by Hilton's recent appraisal of traditional mathematics education in which he highlighted four 'adverse features':

> Broadly speaking, these adverse features may be described as *dehumanization*, *artificiality*, *authoritarianism*, and *dishonesty*. Dehumanization is exemplified by rote calculation and memory dependence; artificiality by spurious applications and contrived problems; authoritarianism by rigid application of formal procedures; and dishonesty by a lack of candor, by unjustifiable attempts at motivation, by imprecise statements and, as with articifiality, by phony applications.[3]

Hilton attempted to substantiate these claims of misanthropy with the following example, involving addition and subtraction of fractions:

> Thus we find in one text "John swims 22 ⅔ metres on Monday and 23 4/7 metres on Tuesday. How far has he swum on the two days?" The application is spurious because John would never *know* that he had swum these fractional distances!...The pedagogy is dishonest, because the attempt is being made to convince the child that he or she needs to learn how to add fractions in order to be able to answer interesting questions...In another text we find "You have ⅔ of a cup of flour and you need ¾ of a cup. How much flour must you add?" In the unlikely event of the cook finding himself or herself in this situation, he or she would obviously simply fill the cup to the ¾ mark – no self-respecting cook would subtract ⅔ from ¾, measure out 1/12 of a cup, and add that to the ⅔ of a cup already measured out.[4]

4 Basic numeracy best antidote to 'anxiety' about mathematics

While it may be true that these examples do not correspond necessarily to 'real life' experiences, nonetheless ought we not to expect children to be *capable* of adding and subtracting such elementary fractions? Moreover, while such problems may not be part of pupils' everyday experiences, they are sufficiently realistic to encourage children to think hypothetically – a useful skill, and one that Hilton failed to consider.

Hilton concluded his somewhat doctrinaire appraisal of traditional mathematics education with the following suggestion:

> We must teach [these] people good, useful mathematics in a low-key, relaxed style, free from authoritarianism, so that they come to feel not threatened by it, not daunted by its unfamiliar symbols, but comfortable with it and convinced that they are now better able to reach rational decisions and cope with our complicated world.[6]

Despite these touching Utopian aspirations, Hilton did not present a shred of evidence that fear of mathematics in adults and children is due to traditional teaching methods. On the contrary, previous research has shown that one of the most effective antidotes to anxiety is basic numeracy. In an extensive study of some 5000 school children, Biggs reported that, by and large, rote learning of arithmetical facts produced significantly less anxiety than more laissez-faire methods based on 'modern' mathematics, lower anxiety was particularly marked for low and average IQ children, and for girls.

5 Advantage of rote learning: creation of automatic response

While rote learning of arithmetic in schools has its origin firmly in the last century, some of the strongest evidence in support of its pedagogic efficacy has been provided by recent psychological research.

For many years number 'facts' were taken to be the most fundamental units of calculation. It was assumed that these were memorised and recalled on demand and that no reasoning or 'mental processing' went on in arriving at the answer. However, recently psychologists have established quite clearly that these most basic calculations can themselves be broken down into mental sub-components with a definite 'information load'. Furthermore, it has been demonstrated that this load can be significantly reduced through practice. Reduction in mental load is known as *automaticity*.

The crux of the automaticity argument may be summed up in the following extract:

> ... while the child should appreciate the manner in which the tables are built up, the facts contained therein should be instantly available to him and it should be possible for him to bring them to mind without thinking. Unless these facts *are* readily available, attention must be given to working them out while 'on the job' and this attention might be better employed in the mathematical activity for which these facts are needed.[7]

Thus, the basic rationale is simple. In solving a mathematical problem there is a limited amount of memory and attention available to the solver. A high level of automaticity for the number facts would free up more memory and attention for coping with more complex aspects of the mathematical problem. On the other hand, if automaticity has not been achieved, then there may be insufficient free memory and attention to cope with these complexities. It would seem, therefore, that there are sound pedagogic grounds for teaching children their tables after all!

6   Myths used to discredit rote learning

As noted previously, arguments against rote learning have tended to consist of unsubstantiated accusations, rather than reasoned claims based on empirical findings. In this section we consider briefly some of the more common myths concerning rote learning.

Myth 1: Children find rote learning boring.
This is perhaps the most frequently stated objection to rote learning, and yet there is simply no evidence that children become bored while reciting tables. Opponents of rote learning claim that chil-

dren have a high level of 'discovery motivation' and that constant repetition of meaningless number facts frustrates this. However, as early as 1922 Thorndike, a great champion of rote learning, had the perspicacity to observe that:

> Computation is not dull if the pupil can compute. He does not object to its barrenness of vital meaning, so long as the barrenness of failure is prevented. We must not forget that pupils like to learn.[8]

Thorndike hits the nail on the head. As any parent knows, children not only have a high 'discovery motivation', they also have an extremely high 'competence motivation' and, as such, they rarely tire of success. We are all familiar with the constant demands of children to hear the same nursery rhyme or bed-time story over and over again, or the constant repetition of the games and jokes in which they delight. Young children also find security in such repetitive behaviour, since the contingencies are very stable, a finding which is consistent with Biggs' observation that rote learning produced lower levels of anxiety than more laissez-faire methods, especially in low and average ability ranges.[9]

Devil's advocacy might lead one to suggest that the introduction of 'modern' methods may have been motivated, not by the fact that children become bored with rote learning, but rather that it is the parents and teachers who tire of such repetition! This suggestion would also be consistent with the current popularity of computer-administered drill and practice routines which have made rote learning more fashionable again, and which neither parents, teachers nor children seem to find boring!

Myth 2: Continuous repetition induces tendencies to perform slavishly and impairs conceptual understanding.
Empirical evidence in support of this view is at best patchy and more recent studies suggest quite the opposite. Thiele reported that 'discovery' was superior to rote learning.[10] However, Pincus observed no such difference,[11] and Anderson reported that lower IQ children benefitted particularly from rote learning.[12] Howard and Norman found no difference between 'meaningful' instruction and 'drill' on immediate testing, however, they reported that a com-

bination of meaningful instruction followed by drill was better on delayed testing.[13] Wallen and Travers, strong proponents of 'modern' methods, observed that children using 'progressive' techniques were significantly inferior to those using rote learning up to age 12. Having set out to champion the cause of 'progressive' methods Wallen and Travers could only make the following evasive statement:

> ...reducing the amount of authoritarian control over students does not necessarily result in drastic impairment of their academic skills, contrary to the expectation of many.[14]

An impairment nonetheless! Biggs' extensive study also revealed that, with the possible exception of highly intelligent boys, rote learning was largely superior for arithmetic involving *both* mechanical and conceptual tasks.[15] Traditional methods were also found to be vastly superior for remedial teaching. These findings are entirely consistent with the automaticity argument referred to previously, which suggests that those children who have learned their arithmetical tables would have more 'redundant attention' to devote to conceptual aspects of mathematical tasks.

It would perhaps be fair to argue that, not only does numerical competence aid conceptual understanding, but it is a *necessary* basis for such understanding. The apparent implication of this might be that additional rote learning of tables should be offered to those having difficulty with certain conceptual aspects of mathematical problem solving.

Myth 3: All problems should be concrete and should correspond to children's 'real-life' experiences.
This view corresponds to Hilton's (1981) accusations of 'artificiality' and 'dishonesty' referred to previously.[16] The fallaciousness of these views was highlighted some 50 years previous by Ballard who wrote:

> It was believed that children hated multiplying 5247 by 78, but if they were allowed to write the word 'apples', or 'elephants', or 'bales of cotton' after the 5247, they would regard the multiplying as a privilege and joy. It was weariness to the flesh to reduce five hundredweights to ounces, but to reduce five hundred-

weights of coal to ounces was as cheery a business as reducing them to ashes...

All we have to do, then, is boycott the mechanical sum and let our youngsters wallow in problems. Unfortunately they refuse to wallow. They find the problem no more to their liking than the mechanical sum. Indeed, less so. Let the reader ask a number of school-children which they prefer, a straightforward sum (children always call it that) or a problem, and he will find that two out of every three will say they prefer the straightforward sum.

...We must face the cold fact that arithmetic, however much it is doctored or dressed up, is not an interesting subject to the ordinary child.

...Fortunately, there is one thing that all pupils like, and that is success.[17]

7   Advocates of 'modern' mathematics should shoulder blame for high levels of innumeracy

In this chapter, we have considered briefly some of the arguments for and against the teaching of arithmetic tables by rote to young children. It would appear that the advantages of rote learning far outweigh more laissez-faire methods through which the young child is encouraged to discover arithmetical facts and rules through investigation, practical acitvity, and such like. While not denying that these methods are undoubtedly extremely useful pedagogic strategies for later learning, there are a number of important caveats.

Firstly, such activities should be founded in a solid base of arithmetical competence achieved through rote learning of tables. Secondly, discovery methods should not be encouraged for young children. Instead, these pupils should be taught using clearly defined contingencies, rather than being allowed to direct their own activities. Furthermore, it should be acknowledged that automaticity in the number facts is a necessary basis for subsequent conceptual understanding. It should also be recognised that children do not suffer boredom through repetition, so long as they are operating at a reasonable level of success.

As noted at the beginning of this chapter, the level of innumeracy in the UK (and other countries) has led to an unprecedented level of concern amongst politicians, educators, employers and parents. Proponents of 'modern' mathematics must shoulder much of the blame. Having objected to traditional methods on the grounds that they produced children with a veneer of numeracy hiding a basic lack of understanding of mathematics, the advocates of 'new maths' produced a generation of mathematical incompetents without even this veneer of numeracy. This was due in part to the ill-founded notion that children could be taught understanding, rather than the means through which understanding might be allowed to develop.

8 'Modern' mathematics precludes parental assistance

Perhaps more fundamentally, 'modern' mathematics had the effect of alienating parents. Highly motivated mothers and fathers, who previously were quite prepared to give their children extra practice on their tables, suddenly found themselves grappling with sets, relations, and the like. Naturally these parents were reluctant to become involved, partly because they were intimidated by the 'new maths', and partly because they were afraid of undoing all the good work [sic] of the teacher by telling their child something 'wrong'. Indeed, mathematics was not the only subject from which parents were alienated. Few will forget the infamous 'phonetic' alphabet which produced large numbers of semi-literate school leavers, and which made parents reluctant even to ask their children to say the alphabet.

9 Basic numeracy crucial first stage of mathematical understanding

Sadly, we seem not to have learned much from these mistakes. It is bewildering and regrettable that the Cockcroft Report has rejected the notion of a 'back to basics' approach to mathematics teaching, despite acknowledging the need for a 'bottom-up' curriculum. Having identified the low level of mathematical attainment, it would seem that Cockroft has recommended the continuation of precisely those teaching methods which are at fault.[18] The crisis in mathematics education could be greatly alleviated if primary schools had a simple brief to produce numerate children using traditional methods of rote learning, leaving secondary schools free to develop deeper mathematical understanding safe in the knowledge that their pupils can at least add, subtract, multiply and divide.

Notes and References

1. *The Times*, 3 February, 1987.
2. W.H. Cockroft, *Mathematics Counts*, Report of the Committee of Inquiry into the Teaching of Mathematics, HMSO, 1982.
3. P.J. Hilton, 'Avoiding Math Avoidance', in L.A. Steen (ed.), *Mathematics Tomorrow*, Springer-Verlag, 1981, p. 78.
4. Ibid., pp. 78–79.
5. Ibid., pp. 81–82.
6. J.B. Biggs *Mathematics and the Conditions of Learning*, National Foundation For Educational Research in England and Wales, 1967.
7. A.W. Bell, J. Costello and D.E. Kuchemann, *A Review of Research in Mathematical Education: Research on Learning and Teaching*, Shell Centre for Mathematical Education, University of Nottingham, 1980.
8. E.L. Thorndike, *The Psychology of Arithmetic*, Macmillan, 1922.
9. J.B. Biggs, *Mathematics and the Conditions of Learning*, National Foundation for Educational Research in England and Wales, 1967.
10. C.I. Thiele, *The Contribution of Generalization to the Learning of the Addition Facts*, Teachers' College Bureau of Publications, Columbia University, 1938.
11. M. Pincus, 'An investigation into the effectiveness of two methods of instruction in addition and subtraction facts', *Dissertation Abstracts*, Vol. 16, 1955, p. 1415.
12. G.L. Anderson, 'Quantitative thinking as developed connectionist and field theories of learning', in *Learning Theory in School Situations*, Studies in Education No. 2, University of Minnesota, 1949.
13. C.F. Howard, 'Three methods of teaching arithmetic', *California Journal of Educational Research*, No. 1, pp. 3–7; M. Norman, 'Three methods of teaching basic division facts', *Dissertation Abstracts*, Vol. 15, 1955, p. 2134.
14. N.E. Wallen and R.M.W. Travers, 'Analysis and investigation of teaching methods' in N.F. Gage (ed.) *Handbook of Research on Teaching*, Rand-McNally, 1963.
15. *Mathematics and the Conditions of Learning*, op. cit.
16. *Mathematics Tomorrow*, op. cit.
17. P.B. Ballard, *Teaching the Essentials of Arithmetic*, University of London Press, 1928, pp. 28–33.
18. *Mathematics Counts*, op. cit.

Publications from
The Social Affairs Unit

Collections

FAMILY PORTRAITS

Edited by Digby Anderson and Graham Dawson

Mary Kenny on feminists and the family

Robert Chester on the popularity of the 'normal' family

Patricia Morgan on feminists' attempts to sack fathers

Hermione Parker on government subversion of the family

Duncan Mitchell on artificial reproduction and the future of the family

and *David Marsland* on young people and the state, *Valerie Riches* on permissiveness, *Andrew Brown* on the family in 'permissive' Sweden and *Digby Anderson* and *Graham Dawson* on the popular but unrepresented 'normal' family

ISBN 0 907631 20 7   £4.95

A DIET OF REASON: SENSE AND NONSENSE IN THE HEALTHY EATING DEBATE

Edited by Digby Anderson

'...a complex, sensible and badly needed book'   *New Scientist*

ISBN 0 907631 26 6   Casebound   £9.95
ISBN 0 907631 22 3   Paperback   £5.95

THE WAYWARD CURRICULUM: A CAUSE FOR PARENTS' CONCERN?

Edited by Dennis O'Keeffe

'This excellent collection'   *Times Higher Education Supplement*

ISBN 0 907631 19 3   £9.95 casebound

TRESPASSING? BUSINESSMEN'S VIEWS ON THE EDUCATION SYSTEM

Michael Brophy et al.

'...much of what the industrialists say would be readily embraced by people in the LEAs and activists in the teaching profession'

Education

ISBN 0 907631 11 8   £2.95

HOME TRUTHS

Barbara Robson et al.

'illustrate(s) the need for members to be aware of the chasm that too often yawns between even progressive housing policies and how they work out in practice'   *Local Government Chronicle*

ISBN 0 907631 05 3   £2.95

EDUCATED FOR EMPLOYMENT?

Digby Anderson et al.

'...the [SAU] has turned its attention to the need for a more precisely governed relationship between educator and employer'

Times Higher Educational Supplement

ISBN 0 907631 03 7   £2.65

THE PIED PIPERS OF EDUCATION

Antony Flew et al.

'The SAU has chosen a provocative role in an attempt to improve real debate about the ground rules for education and welfare'

Times Educational Supplement

ISBN 0 907631 02 9   £2.65

CRIMINAL WELFARE ON TRIAL

Colin Brewer et al.

'Its new and astringent mix of pragmatism and genuine social concern...is bound to attract a positive response'   *Church Times*

ISBN 0 907631 01 1   £2.65

BREAKING THE SPELL OF THE WELFARE STATE

Digby Anderson, June Lait & David Marsland

'almost as critical of the present government's strategies as the policies of previous Labour administrations'   *The Guardian*

ISBN 0 907631 00 2   £2.65

Reports – *TAKING THOUGHT FOR THE ENVIRONMENT*

AFTER GOVERNMENT FAILURE?
D.R. Denman
ISBN 0 907631 24 X   £2.50

PLANNING FAILS THE INNER CITIES
R.N. Goodchild & D.R. Denman
ISBN 0 907631 25 8   £2.50

CARING FOR THE COUNTRYSIDE: PUBLIC DEPENDENCE ON PRIVATE INTEREST
Barry Bracewell-Milnes
ISBN 0 907631 27 4   £2.50

'refute the widespread contention that the greatest harm done to the environment is by individuals [and] cite a number of initiatives taken by companies and individuals to safeguard and improve the environment in which they live and work.'   *Financial Times*

Reports – *TAKING THOUGHT FOR THE POOR*

WEALTH AND POVERTY: A JEWISH ANALYSIS
Jonathan Sacks
ISBN 0 907631 15 0   £2.00

THE BIBLE, JUSTICE AND THE CULTURE OF POVERTY: EMOTIVE CALLS TO ACTION VERSUS RATIONAL ANALYSIS
Irving Hexham
ISBN 0 907631 16 9   £2.00

THE PHILOSOPHY OF POVERTY: GOOD SAMARITANS OR PROCRUSTEANS?
Antony Flew
ISBN 0 907631 17 7   £2.00

THE CHRISTIAN RESPONSE TO POVERTY: WORKING WITH GOD'S ECONOMIC LAWS
James Sadowsky
ISBN 0 907631 18 5   £2.00

'An intellectual counter-attack is underway from the Social Affairs Unit.'
The Guardian

Research Reports

THE MEGAPHONE SOLUTION: GOVERNMENT ATTEMPTS TO CURE SOCIAL PROBLEMS WITH MASS MEDIA CAMPAIGNS
Digby Anderson
'...ask[s] the right questions'   *Media Week*
Research Report 9,   ISBN 0 907631 28 2   £3.00

DENYING HOMES TO BLACK CHILDREN
David Dale
'...challenges the view that transracial adoption can be psychologically harmful'   *The Scotsman*
Research Report 8,   ISBN 0 907631 23 1   £3.50

DETERRING POTENTIAL CRIMINALS
Ernest van den Haag
'will most probably have a considerable influence'
Howard Journal of Criminal Justice
Research Report 7,   ISBN 0 907631 14 2   £2.00

ASIAN HOUSING IN BRITAIN
Jon Davies
'...a broadside attack on academic research into immigrant housing'
New Society
Research Report 6,   ISBN 0 907631 13 4   £2.00

REVERSING RACISM: LESSONS FROM AMERICA
Kenneth M. Holland & Geoffrey Parkins
'Britain...warned today against emulating the American pattern of positive discrimination'   *The Times*
Research Report 5,   ISBN 0 907631 10 X   £2.00

ACTION ON WELFARE: REFORM OF PERSONAL INCOME TAXATION AND SOCIAL SECURITY

Hermione Parker

'...represent(s) an important contribution to the debate on social policy the Government cannot ignore'   *The Times*

Research Report 4,   ISBN 0 907631 04 5   £2.00

TRACTS BEYOND THE TIMES: A BRIEF GUIDE TO THE COMMUNIST OR REVOLUTIONARY MARXIST PRESS

Charles Ellwell

'I can warmly recommend it...a valuable guide'   Bernard Levin
The Times

Research Report 3,   ISBN 0 907631 08 8   £1.50

ARE THE POLICE FAIR? NEW LIGHT ON THE SOCIOLOGICAL EVIDENCE

P.A.J. Waddington

'Sociologists rapped for anti-police bias'   *Sociological Review*

Research Report 2,   ISBN 0 907631 07 X   £1.00

ARE THE POLICE UNDER CONTROL?

David Regan

'a good case'   *Daily Telegraph*

Research Report 1,   ISBN 0 907631 06 1   £1.00

Monographs

DETECTING BAD SCHOOLS: A GUIDE FOR NORMAL PARENTS

Digby Anderson

'combines sense with humour…never dull…if it alerts parents to their rights…and reminds teachers of their responsibilities to parents, it can do a lot of good'   *Universe*

ISBN 0 907631 04 5   £1.00

EXTRA DRY: COLUMNS IN THE TIMES

Digby Anderson

'imperative writing on political and social subjects'

The Spectator

ISBN 0 907631 12 6   £2.95

Books

THE KINDNESS THAT KILLS: THE CHURCHES' SIMPLISTIC RESPONSE TO COMPLEX SOCIAL ISSUES
Edited by Digby Anderson

'an excellent point of reference…sets out succinctly the feebleness, predictability, ignorance and uncharitableness of so many church productions'
Charles Moore, The Spectator

Commissioned by the SAU and published by SPCK
ISBN 0 281 04096 6   £3.95

Studies in Social Revaluation
EDUCATIONAL ACHIEVEMENT IN JAPAN: LESSONS FOR THE WEST
Richard Lynn

'a timely publication, offering statistical evidence of Japan's higher educational standards through international comparison'
Times Educational Supplement

Published in co-operation with The Macmillan Press
Casebound: ISBN 0 333 44531 7   £29.50
Paperback: ISBN 0 333 44532 5   £8.95

FROM CRADLE TO GRAVE: COMPARATIVE PERSPECTIVES ON THE STATE OF WELFARE
Ralph Segalman and David Marsland

Published in co-operation with The Macmillan Press
Casebound: ISBN 0 333 47004 4
Paperback: ISBN 0 333 47005 2

The Social Affairs Unit